Manitoba's Most Notorious True Crimes

CRIMES
of the CENTURY

Bibliothèque Régionale JOLYS Regional Library
Box 113
St-Pierre-Jolys, Manitoba
R0A 1V0

Manitoba's Most Notorious True Crimes

CRIMES
of the CENTURY

Bill Redekop

GREAT PLAINS PUBLICATIONS

Copyright © 2002 Bill Redekop

Great Plains Publications
420 – 70 Arthur Street
Winnipeg, MB R3B 1G7
www.greatplains.mb.ca

All rights reserved. No part of this publication may be reproduced or transmitted in any form or in any means, or stored in a database and retrieval system, without the prior written permission of Great Plains Publications, or, in the case of photocopying or other reprographic copying, a license from CANCOPY (Canadian Copyright Licensing Agency), 6 Adelaide Street East, Suite 900, Toronto, Ontario, Canada, M5C 1H6.

Great Plains Publications gratefully acknowledges the financial support provided for its publishing program by the Government of Canada through the Book Publishing Industry Development Program (BPIDP); the Canada Council for the Arts; the Manitoba Department of Culture, Heritage and Tourism; and the Manitoba Arts Council.

Design & Typography by Gallant Design Ltd.
Printed in Canada by Friesens

CANADIAN CATALOGUING IN PUBLICATION DATA

Main entry under title:

Redekop, Bill
Crimes of the century

ISBN 1-894283-34-1

Crime – Manitoba – History – 20th century.   2. Criminals – Manitoba – History – 2th century.   I. Title
HV6809.M3R42   2002   364.1'097127'0904   C2002-910618-4

To Mary

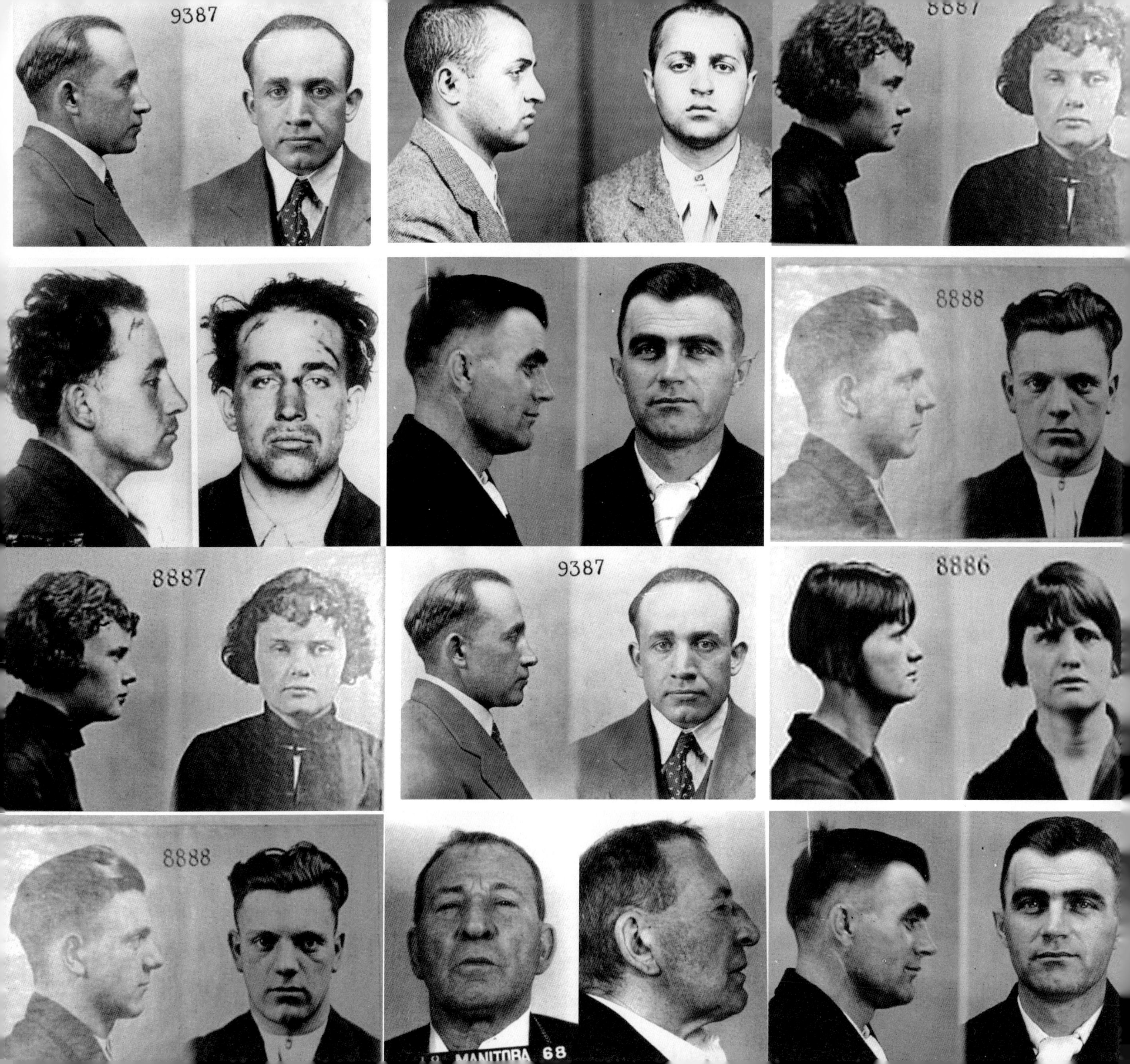
9387
8887
8888
8887
9387
8886
8888
MANITOBA 68

CONTENTS

WOMAN ON THE GALLOWS
EMILY HILDA BLAKE
1

DEATH OF A LADY'S MAN
BLOODY JACK KRAFCHENKO
15

BOOZE, GLORIOUS BOOZE!
BILL WOLCHOCK AND PROHIBITION IN MANITOBA
31

THE STRANGLER
EARLE (THE GORILLA) NELSON
47

THE GREAT GOLD ROBBERY
FLYING BANDIT KEN LEISHMAN
67

THE MYSTERIOUS MR. KASSER
ALEXANDER KASSER AND THE CFI
91

THE CASE OF THE KILLER COPS
BARRY NIELSEN AND JERRY STOLAR
109

THE SEARCH FOR ABORIGINAL JUSTICE
HELEN BETTY OSBORNE AND J.J. HARPER
121

PREFACE

BRITISH ORPHAN HILDA BLAKE FEARED HER LIFE WAS SLIPPING INTO OBSCURITY WHEN SHE MURDERED HER HOUSE MISTRESS AT THE TURN OF THE 20TH CENTURY IN BRANDON.

Earle Nelson liked to read about his exploits in newspapers as one of North America's first serial killers. That included a June 8, 1927 edition of the *Manitoba Free Press* found in his coat pocket after a grisly murder spree in Winnipeg.

Ken Leishman was the criminal genius behind the Great Gold Robbery at Winnipeg International Airport on March 1, 1966, yet his undoing was to boast about it to a cell mate who turned out to be an undercover RCMP officer.

If I couldn't see the thread connecting these and other Manitoba crimes of the century, retired University of Winnipeg criminology professor William Morrison surely could. The common thread? Ego. Spot the ego. Then you begin to understand the motive behind the crime.

Morrison recited a simple rule of thumb among criminologists: when people can't get attention by doing something good, they resort to doing something bad. And if they still can't get attention by doing bad things, they resort to doing very bad things, sometimes even murder.

That's one of the themes in *Crimes of the Century*. The book invites a certain amount of amateur sleuthing—we're all experts on ego—but it's also about Manitoba history, and it's also about catharsis. Crimes are part of history but some illustrate history more than others, like the tale of Manitoba's biggest bootlegger Bill Wolchock. The story of Wolchock, and his liquor export business to gangsters like Al Capone in Chicago and Kid Cann in Minneapolis, depicts the social upheaval caused by liquor and its prohibition in the 1920s and 1930s. Yet Wolchock, a blue collar worker, would provide work and living wages to more than 30 other unemployed workers during the height of the Great Depression. Was Wolchock a criminal? The federal government thought so. Wolchock would spend five years behind bars for income tax evasion. Wolchock's story is told here for the first time.

Then there is catharsis in the pain caused by many of the criminals, starting with serial killer Nelson. Writers on serial killers often display a black humour towards the crimes, especially when more than half a century has passed. Not here. Nelson was killing the women of Manitoba and he haunts us still.

That's it for this introduction. I'd like to thank the staff at Great Plains Publications, especially Jewls Dengl who conceptualized this book and Douglas Allen who contributed the sidebar stories. In closing, I have but one request of you, the dear and virtuous reader: don't get any ideas.

ACKNOWLEDGEMENTS

Special thanks to the *Winnipeg Free Press* and librarian Lynn Crothers.

Thanks also to Mark Campbell, Pauline and Cyril Deane, Ray Fetterly, Wayne Glowacki, Ron Godfrey, Colin Goff, Larry Halcro, Cleo Heinrichs, Mary Herd, Reinhold Kramer, Wally Landreth, Blair Leishman, Ron Leishman, Kelly Main, Glen Matheson, Mike McIntyre, Tom Mitchell, William Morrison, Dorothy Penner, Isaac and Margaret Redekop, Paul Redekop, Red Lake Museum, James Ritchie, Kathryn Ritchot, Randy Rostecki, Doug Skoog, Rick Smit, Staff Sgt. Jack Templeman, Ray Wehner, Len Wolchock, and Martin Zeilig.

CHAPTER 1

WOMAN ON THE GALLOWS

EMILY HILDA BLAKE

There has always been great sympathy for Emily Hilda Blake, the only woman ever hanged in Manitoba. Police sniffled during her arrest. Guards and other witnesses choked back tears at her execution. Even today she evokes strong emotions.

"She's our Tess," said Brandon University historian Tom Mitchell, comparing Blake to Thomas Hardy's fictitious heroine Tess of D'Ubervilles. Mitchell and colleague Reinhold Kramer co-authored *Walk Towards the Gallows: The Tragedy of Hilda Blake*, which uses the Blake case to explore the social history of the times.

"She's a very tragic person. She was courageous. She walked up the gallows steps and let them put a rope on her, whereas the men often had to be carried up," Mitchell said in an interview.

And yet...

In the late afternoon of July 5, 1899, in the comfortable home of Brandon businessman Robert Lane, housemaid Hilda Blake kissed her employer's pregnant young wife, then fired a revolver into her back. Mrs. Mary Lane, shot through the left lung, staggered into the front yard where her four children played at serving tea. She wheezed her last breath before she could utter her killer's name.

Blake was 21 that fateful summer day in 1899 and had worked for Robert and Mary Lane for just over a year. The Lane family, in today's terms, was upwardly mobile. Robert Lane, 36, was a hardworking entrepreneur. He was co-partner in Brandon's largest transfer company with 30 teams of horses, and controlled

CRIMES OF THE CENTURY

Young, pretty, strong-willed, intelligent—so news reports of the day said—there was much about Hilda Blake, in turn-of-the-century Brandon, to fascinate Manitobans.

the city's block-ice trade. He had married up socially when he betrothed Mary Robinson. Robert and Mary, 32, had four children. Employing a servant was part of their rising status.

Blake was the only witness to the shooting of Mary Lane. Blake claimed a tramp with a foreign accent came to the door asking for food. She said Mary Lane refused him and the beggar shot her in the back. The CPR tracks ran behind their property and tramps riding the rails were a regular nuisance. The public swallowed Blake's story wholly. No woman could commit such a crime. The killing of a pregnant mother right in her own home sent shock waves across the country. In southwestern Manitoba, armed vigilante groups blocked off all roads into Brandon and roamed the countryside rounding up tramps. Mobs railed against the country's immigration policies.

But Blake's story, which fed the prejudice against hoboes and immigrants, was too convenient for Brandon Police Chief James Kircaldy. He knew Mary Lane could not have been shot from where Blake claimed because there were burn marks on Mary's dress indicating the gun was just inches away. He also learned that a woman fitting Hilda Blake's description had purchased a revolver in Winnipeg several weeks earlier, the same revolver later found hidden in the Lane's yard. Confronted with the evidence, Blake offered little resistance and quickly confessed.

Young, pretty, strong-willed, intelligent—so news reports of the day said—there was much about Hilda Blake, in turn-of-the-century Brandon, to fascinate Manitobans. She was also head-strong, fanciful, prone to depression, and lost. Lost because she was one of tens of thousands of British orphan children transported to Canada following the untimely deaths of their parents. From 1869 to 1925, 80,000 orphans arrived in Canada. These boat children were little more than unpaid servants in many households. Blake lost her parents, country, social standing, education, and was dropped into a harsh prairie landscape when she was just 11 years old.

One of her first acts upon arriving on a farm near Kola, north of Brandon, was to run away, perhaps not from anyone or anything except fortune's yoke. A neighbour took her in and Blake became the centre of a custody battle. She eventually returned to the original family of Alfred P. Stewart, finding life with the second family even more unbearable. After several years with the Stewarts she moved on, drifting around Manitoba, including Winnipeg, working from household to household as a maidservant. Former employers praised her handling of children. They also said she suffered depression, although it is not known if it was clinical depression or a kind of emotional despair at her predicament.

The murder was a whodunit for four days; it's been a "why-she-dunit" for more than a century. Blake never gave a satisfactory

The Lanes were a prominent family in the fast-growing city of Brandon.

explanation as to why she killed Mary Lane. She told Kircaldy she was jealous of Mary Lane and loved the children, as if she planned to simply take her place. She also claimed she was despairing and suicidal at the time, suggesting it was a toss up who to kill, herself or Mary Lane. Her reasons didn't seem adequate to the public, and some people speculated there had been a rendezvous between Hilda Blake and Robert Lane. That includes Brandon University professors Mitchell and Kramer.

The speculation was abetted by a poem Blake wrote two weeks before her execution, titled "My Downfall." Quite sophisticated for

CRIMES OF THE CENTURY

"The girl said she had no ill-will towards the deceased, but in fact, was very comfortable in the house, and evidently fond of the children..."

someone with little formal education, the poem describes a metaphorical man luring the writer into temptation.

> ...one day the devil, in the form of a man,
> Came smiling towards me; said he, "You can
>   Know more, if you'll take them,
> Of joy and pleasures," I heard him say,
> "Then e'er you have dreamed of; I'll show you
>   the way."

Mitchell and Kramer believe Blake is pointing the finger at Robert Lane as her seducer and the one responsible for her downfall. They argue Blake never blamed Lane directly in order to protect him. In fact, Blake never complained about how the Lanes treated her. "The girl said she had no ill-will towards the deceased, but in fact, was very comfortable in the house, and evidently fond of the children," the *Winnipeg Telegram* said.

Is the poem sexual in nature? Are those the pleasures Blake refers to several times? Mitchell and Kramer certainly think so. If they are sexual references, it could indicate Blake had been sexually abused as a child. When sex is mixed into a crime it often indicates a history of child abuse, say psychologists. If a person is able to murder someone, it demonstrates an inability to feel compassion for other people. That comes from basic trust being destroyed. According to most psychologists, child abuse breaks down trust. Mitchell and Kramer point to the potential for sexual abuse against someone so young cast out in the world. They say being a domestic servant was dangerous work for women at the turn of the century. Birth statistics from the period show a high percentage of the babies born out of wedlock were to servant women. Neither would Blake have confessed to being sexually abused. That just wasn't done a century ago.

Mitchell and Kramer discovered that two months before her murder, Mary Lane returned home to Birtle to visit her family. Robert Lane and Blake were alone in the house for at least three weeks together. What happened during those three weeks?

Blake also penned a last-minute autobiography that Mitchell and Kramer argue accuses Robert Lane of being a sexual predator. The manuscript worked its way up the provincial and federal justice systems all the way to Governor General Gilbert John Minto and finally Prime Minister Wilfrid Laurier. The manuscript prompted Minto to plead clemency for Blake, in a letter to Laurier:

"If her own confession (autobiography) is accepted against herself, that confession lays bare the most horrible story I have ever read against (Robert) Lane," the Governor General wrote, "...To execute her, would appear I should have thought logically to compel (sic) his execution too...According to her confession, it was Lane's influence that was answerable for the murder and it seems to have been a shabby mean influence, evidently intended to save himself, while she is bent on saving him."

Laurier denied clemency, at a time when death sentences against women were usually commuted.

"Robert Lane was probably a very conventional guy. The fact that he made a domestic servant a sexual partner isn't necessarily news," maintained Mitchell. Perhaps Lane told Blake he wished he could be with her if not for his marriage, said Mitchell. "How many men have said that to a woman? I think Hilda Blake fell in love with Robert Lane. I think he gave her encouragement. And she had enough gumption to pull off something that almost worked."

However, the argument that Blake was a victim of a male-dominated society is not foolproof. Sexual abuse could have occurred within Blake's adoptive family in southwestern Manitoba, yet her adopted father regularly came to see her while she was in prison. Blake remarked on his kindness in a letter to the police chief Kircaldy. That doesn't sound like the act of a man guilty of sexually abusing his adopted daughter. Blake left the family in her early teens and worked across Manitoba as a servant in several households. Exploitation for sex could have occurred then.

Also, the greatest condemnation in the poem written by Blake is for society generally, the seemingly upright society of turn-of-the-century Brandon and southwestern Manitoba, for doing so little to prevent her

• Mary and Robert Lane

BIG BAD JOHN

PERSONNEL

When it comes to larger than life figures, they don't come much larger than John S. Ingram. When Ingram arrived in frontier Winnipeg in 1873, he quickly discovered that it was his kind of town. Plenty of raucous saloons, lots of gambling houses, and a goodly number of pretty girls employed in the oldest profession. Ingram loved his women, he loved his wine, but most of all, he loved a good old barroom brawl. His scraps in various saloons were legendary, and there is no evidence of his ever losing.

Eventually, John joined the recently expanded North West Mounted Police force, which was the sole keeper of law and order in the province. Although he was adept with firearms he rarely bothered to carry one, preferring to make his arrests by simply pummelling the offender into submission. By all accounts, his rather crude method of establishing law and order was effective, particularly in frontier Winnipeg. Legend has it that he arrested Ambroise Lepine, Louis Riel's Adjutant-General in the provisional government of 1869-70, who was charged with murder in the Thomas Scott execution, with a one punch knockout.

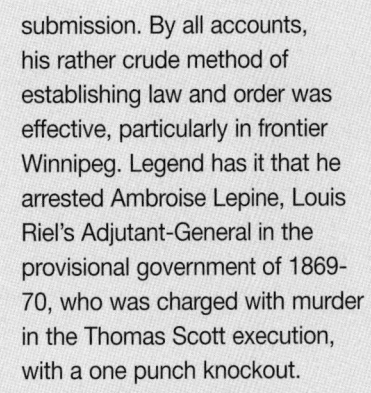

In 1874, the recently incorporated city of Winnipeg chose John S. Ingram as its first chief. Big John went right to work. His first item of business was to rid the town of the criminal element. Within a short period, these petty thieves left town on the end of Ingram's knuckles, or found another line of endeavour.

Ingram's next task was a bit more delicate. He knew that it would be impossible to eliminate prostitution. After all, even in the Wild West one couldn't go around cold-cocking members of the fairer sex. So Ingram adopted the policy of containment. The trade centred in an area of the west end, in the vicinity of Minto Street. Ingram's policy was simple. Stay in that area, stay in line, and there would be no trouble from the police. For a time this appeared to satisfy all, particularly Big John, as he was a frequent "visitor" to this area of town.

However, this cozy arrangement was not to last. Ingram became besotted with the gals at one particular house, and spent more and more time there. Public murmurings of misconduct became more voluble, and the Presbyterian element of city council began agitating for an all out effort to stamp out prostitution. There were suggestions that Ingram was running a protection racket, which offended Ingram no end.

Matters came to a head in 1875. Two of Winnipeg's finest conducted a raid, and who should come up wriggling in the net but Chief John S. Ingram! Frontier justice was swift. The following day Ingram appeared before Mayor Cornish, who was also the city magistrate, and no friend to Ingram. Cornish fined him $8, and Ingram resigned. There was more than a little irony, and some of Ingram's supporters believed more than mere coincidence, that he was replaced by David B. Murray, one of the constables who had arrested him. So ended the brief but colourful career of Winnipeg's first police chief.

For most men, this would have been the final entry in the history books. John S. Ingram was not a man to let a little disgrace diminish him. In 1884, the city of Calgary needed a no-nonsense law man to handle the flood of transients that were pouring in and out of the city, many of whom were cowboys still packing six-guns. Ingram's exploits were well known to city council, and with some trepidation, council hired Ingram as their first chief. True to form, he reprised his Winnipeg performance by pounding and hounding the crooks into the lock-up, or to the city limits.

The similarity to the Winnipeg scenario didn't end there either. No sooner had Calgary become a relatively law abiding town than the editor of the *Calgary Herald* went after Ingram. His campaigning to get rid of the chief finally forced Ingram's resignation, and he left town. The news travelled fast, and within two months Calgary was once again one of the toughest and lawless towns in the west.

Now surely, Ingram's law enforcement career would end here. Wrong. Rossland, B.C., a roaring mining town came a courtin'. Would Ingram consider coming to Rossland to rebuild its police force? Why, certainly. Once again, Ingram smashed his way through every town tough stupid enough to challenge him, and Rossland became as orderly and safe as a mining town could be in those days. And it stayed that way.

So much so that Ingram grew bored, and resigned in 1903. To whet his appetite for action, he became a "dynamite man" for a local mining company, an occupation that required him to prepare fuses for the miners. On December 17, 1905, the main powder blew the mining shack sky-high, injuring 20 nearby miners. Unfortunately, Ingram was in the shack.

Ingram lived big, and died big, and there is no more colourful character in the early history of Winnipeg.

• Winnipeg's first police chief, John S. Ingram.

downfall. The loss of her parents, being sent first to an orphanage, separated from her siblings, and finally being shipped across the ocean, could have also broken down Blake's trust in people.

> *You hypocrites, pleading religion,*
> *You inquisitive seekers of fame,*
> *Ready now with your good advices*
> *When I've drunk of the sorrow and shame;*
> *You gave me no timely warning,*
> *You held out no helping hand,—*
> *Why didn't you see me sinking*
> *As I stepped on the treacherous sand?*

As well, Blake's autobiography that Mitchell and Kramer believe indicts Robert Lane hasn't been seen in a hundred years. Mitchell and Kramer base their assumption of its contents purely on Minto's reaction. The *Brandon Western Sun*, which published her poem, saw the autobiography and refused to run it, saying it would "hardly stand publishing." What this means remains a mystery. Some suggest there may have been legal consequences to publishing it. However, it would not have been libelous if the document accused Lane, only libelous if it named other people not directly involved in the case, and that could have been edited out. Mitchell and Kramer argue it never ran because power-broker Clifford Sifton feared it would jeopardize his pro-immigration policies. Sifton was a newspaper baron of several papers including the *Western Sun* and the *Manitoba Free Press*, while at the same time serving as Ottawa's minister of the interior.

It may simply be that Blake's autobiography was so outlandish that it raised questions about her state of mind. No one can say for sure because the autobiography no longer seems to exist. Mitchell and Kramer filed numerous access to information requests, without success.

Was Hilda Blake crazy? This is what Lane descendants maintain. They say Blake misconstrued Robert Lane's kindness. Mitchell and Kramer dismiss this argument because Blake showed no evidence of mental problems before, and was fully functional in the Lane household and other households where she had worked. Housemaids were around family so much that any mental illness would have been detected, they insist.

There is also a reluctance to say Blake was insane because it ends our fascination with the case. No more amateur sleuthing. The century-old mystery is over.

Not necessarily. Today, Blake's case might be filed under extreme infatuation and stalker phenomena. These syndromes have surfaced in people who seem perfectly normal until they are rejected in some real or imagined relationship. They are still highly unexplained phenomena, yet modern jail cells are full of cases, mostly men. There is no consensus as to the cause. But clearly, Blake's plan that she could kill Mary Lane and simply take her place as mother to the children, and wife to Robert Lane, is classic stalking behaviour, according to criminal psychological profilers like John Douglas, former chief of the FBIs Investigative Support Unit. Stalking is "the magical thinking that if one fact is changed, the stalker and the object of his (or her) 'affection' can enjoy a life together," writes Douglas, in *Anatomy of Motive*.

"The deadly stage is reached when the stalker finally thinks, 'If I can't have her (or him), no one else can,'" according to Douglas.

Of all the various stalking syndromes, de Clérambault's Syndrome, also called erotomania, fits closest with Blake's symptoms. French physician Gaetan de Clérambault (1872-1934) categorized this mental disorder whereby the patient, usually a woman, has an intense delusional belief, including erotic delusions, that a man, usually of a higher social class, is in love with her. The patient believes the object of her infatuation cannot be happy without her. This belief is completely unshakable, no matter how hard the person denies the woman or tries to ignore her. In fact, de Clérambault finished his research completely frustrated by what little success he had treating patients. Whether the object of the patient's affection is married is a mute point for the patient. The patient believes the object of her desire simply cannot live without her. The onslaught of the erotomania can be sudden and overpowering in the patient.

The de Clérambault patient often suffers from depression, and is unlikely to have friends. (Blake suffered depression and was said to be friendless, although Mitchell and Kramer maintain servants had little opportunity to make friends because they worked six days a week and half days on Sunday.) The patient invariably believes the object of her desire is communicating to her by sending secret signals. This might explain the unaddressed letter Blake wrote just weeks before her execution, which was found with her prison matron Emma Stripp. Blake seemed to be writing to someone, presumably

SOUTHERN MANITOBA MASSACRE

Tragedy shattered the small Mennonite village of Altona on October 9, 1902, when teacher Heinrich J. Toews opened fire in his classroom, wounding three small children, one fatally, and three school trustees. Dead was seven-year-old Anna Kehler. Toews then turned the gun on himself but survived. When he recovered, albeit blinded, he wailed at what he had done.

"My sin is greater than that it can be forgiven," Toews cried.

His brother Bernard tried to comfort him with a quote from Isaiah 1:18: "Though your sins be as scarlet, they shall be white as snow; though they be red like crimson, they shall be as wool."

Heinrich Toews asked his brother to go to each house affected by his actions and beg forgiveness, which he did. Several members of the community visited the murderer to give forgiveness, and to pray and read scripture with him. Toews said he had heard an evil voice instruct him to carry out the shooting rampage, but could remember little else of the incident.

He died on January 19, 1903, before his case could go to trial. The reverend at his funeral compared Toews to the penitent thief on the cross who begged that Jesus "remember me when you enter your kingdom." Jesus replied, "This day shalt thou be with me in Paradise."

She maintained, in a Letter to the Editor in the Manitoba Free Press *that followed, that Blake, in her opinion, suffered from "moral insanity"* ...

Robert Lane, about some note sent to her. The implication in Blake's letter is that Lane sent her a message, and she is responding. Yet it seems unlikely Lane would risk sending her any sign of affection, especially if he was in any way culpable.

Blake wrote in the letter: "Now I feel ashamed of myself to be obliged to confess that even that little note has comforted me. You have a strong influence over me knowing as I do how wicked and dishonorable you can be to allow myself to be comforted by the thought that you have taken the trouble to be worried about me. How I do wish to see your face. But I knew you were near and endangering yourself for my sake. Now I shall be comparatively happy for a time longer." Is Blake imagining Lane is in love with her?

Then there is the kiss Blake gave Mary Lane before shooting her. It was not a perfunctory kiss. Blake said Mary Lane's reaction was one of surprise. "She wondered what was the matter with me," Blake said in her confession to police. A Judas kiss of betrayal? It amounted to that, but it was initiated by Blake, not done to avoid raising suspicion like Judas. It seems it was Blake's way of saying sorry. Mary Lane was innocent. Blake didn't have a bad word to say about her. Mary Lane was just in her way. The kiss was strangely heartfelt on Blake's part. Authors Mitchell and Kramer maintain Blake was fixated on rising in social status, just as de Clérambault patients are fixated on a love interest in a higher social stratum. Blake was making her move up the social ladder. It demonstrates an objectifying of Mary Lane that is also a trait of erotomanic patients—to not view a victim as human. We can never know now. But somehow Blake was able to square killing an innocent, pregnant mother of four young children for the completely delusional notion that she could take her place.

One interesting visitor to Blake's death cell was Dr. Amelia Yeomans, a Women's Christian Temperance Union leader and early feminist. One of the first female doctors in Canada, Yeomans planned to spend several days interviewing Blake, hoping to strike up the cause that Blake was a victim of male-dominated society. But the meeting didn't go as planned.

Blake wouldn't take Yeomans' arguments seriously. Blake didn't seem to view her predicament in terms of feminism. Certainly an abuse victim, especially one facing the gallows, might jump at the chance to lay blame elsewhere, like at the male-dominated society or the class structure. However, it may be that Blake just wanted a better position in that class system. Yeomans cut short her visit. She maintained, in a Letter to the Editor in the *Manitoba Free Press* that followed, that Blake, in her opinion, suffered from "moral insanity," which she defined as "the lack of coordination between mental and moral faculties." Yeomans also claimed Blake had "a most irrational self-

PYRO ON THE LOOSE

ARSON

Arson is the costliest of all criminal behaviour, surpassing even fraud in dollar value. In the late 1990s, the Winnipeg Police and Fire Departments were forced to establish an arson squad to deal with the growing number of deliberately set fires plaguing the city. They had their hands full, but nothing close to what their colleagues of 1911 had to contend with.

That fall, one James Dodds began an arson spree unequalled in the city's history. Dodds eventually admitted to starting some one hundred fires, with losses authorities estimated to have exceeded $1,000,000 in value. On one day alone, the fire department responded to 16 alarms. The blazes appeared to be random acts, and along with several commercial buildings in the downtown area, four houses on Home Street were also torched.

The most serious incident occurred at the Radford and Wright warehouse. As fire-fighters were attempting to contain the inferno, there was a large explosion. Four civilians and two fire-fighters were killed, and many others injured.

In arson for profit, the perpetrator makes every effort to conceal the origin of the fire, and either flees the scene immediately, or, more usually, hires someone else to light the match. Dodds, however, was a classic pyromaniac. Not only did he start the fires himself, in many cases he was the one who turned in the alarm. He also had a habit of remaining at the scene and assisting fire-fighters. He was at the scene of the Radford and Wright fire, and on one occasion climbed onto the roof of a burning building, and chopped a hole in the roof for fire-fighters.

Dodds was finally apprehended at the scene of a stable fire on Fort Street. After pleading guilty to 25 charges of arson, Dodds was sentenced to 15 years imprisonment. Manslaughter charges were stayed when it became apparent that Dodds was mentally unfit to stand trial. After a brief stint at the Brandon Mental Institution, Dodds was deported to Scotland, and the entire fire department breathed a sigh of relief.

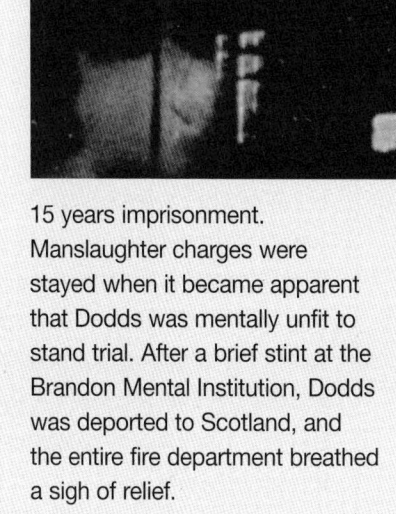

CRIMES OF THE CENTURY

Robert Lane was a nice man, a quiet man, a church-goer, a man careful not to drink to excess, according to existing accounts.

importance." An elevated opinion of oneself fits precisely with de Clérambault patients. Nonetheless, Yeomans began to petition that Blake be spared the executioner.

Ron Godfrey becomes exasperated with suggestions that Blake was mentally ill. For 50 years Godfrey has lived in the 10th Avenue Brandon home where Hilda Blake shot Mary Lane. Godfrey demonstrated where Mary Lane was standing in what was then the dining room, when Hilda Blake shot her. By Blake's account to police, she completely missed with the first shot, never having handled a gun before. So the second time she put the gun right into Mary Lane's back.

"Mary Lane was over here by this wall hanging curtains," explained Godfrey. "One bullet went into the ceiling over there. I may have drywalled over it or the police removed it, I don't know. I didn't even know about the murder at the time."

Not unlike Jesse James, who was hanging a picture when he was shot by Bob Ford. "Except that fella did it for the reward," Godfrey said.

"I don't think she was insane by any means. When I was young, a girl turned me down and I got out the carving knife. I was going to commit suicide. I bet that's happened to 80 per cent of the population.

"I think she was unbalanced because of romance. I think he may have praised her up a bit, but I'm the type of fella who has to see something proven before I'll say they had an affair."

Blake's sanity was never examined. She refused legal counsel. At her hearing, she asked for the harshest penalty. She did not in any serious way try to stop the hanging.

Robert Lane was a nice man, a quiet man, a church-goer, a man careful not to drink to excess, according to existing accounts. He was also handsome and hard-working, descendants of the family maintain. Mary's family, the Robinsons, remained loyal to him, not the behaviour of people who suspected their son-in-law of hanky-panky with the maid. And Lane in turn was good to the Robinson family. He even put up room and board years later for nieces from the Robinson family so they could attend school in Brandon. The predatory male stereotype put forward by Mitchell and Kramer remains quite possible, but it is harder to believe.

Glen Matheson lives in Brandon and is a descendant of the Robinson family. Robert Lane was his great, great uncle. Matheson swore he would say if he thought Lane had taken advantage of Blake, but he doesn't believe he did.

"What I heard growing up was that Uncle Robert was just the most wonderful man to everyone, to the children, and to both sides of the family. It could have been Uncle Robert was nice to her like he was to everybody," said Matheson.

"I think she was completely in love with him, and she was in love with the kids, and wanted them at any cost."

13

Mary's parents John and Anne Robinson moved in with Robert to help care for the children. Mary's father John Robinson was devastated by her murder and died within six months. "He just gave up," Matheson said.

Just over a year after his wife's death, Robert Lane, with four small children, remarried a woman 22 years old, 15 years his junior. They had seven more children together.

Hilda Blake had a strong effect on the public. At her arrest, when she said her emotional good-bye to the Lane children, a reporter wrote that police officers were teary-eyed. Men at her hanging reacted similarly. The irony is that while there were gross inequalities between the sexes, with women not even allowed to vote, men still placed women on pedestals. From newspaper accounts, the woman didn't fit the crime. "A girl of most prepossessing appearance," said the *Manitoba Free Press*, who "has...a good reputation."

Neighbours, who had seen how good Blake was with the Lane children, were the last to believe she could have committed the murder. In Winnipeg, a petition for clemency was placed in the *Manitoba Free Press* office by Yeomans, and its signatures included Winnipeg's mayor A. J. Andrews, and Rodmond P. Roblin, who would become Conservative Premier of Manitoba the next year. It was to no avail. The execution was scheduled for the morning of Dec. 27.

Excerpts from the next day's edition of the *Manitoba Morning Free Press* read: "The drop fell at twenty minutes to nine...Her demeanor during the ordeal was no less wonderful than her remarkable fortitude since the death sentence was passed upon her...She walked steadily to the top (of the scaffold) and then turned and looked searchingly into the faces below."

Blake asked to speak to Alexander McIlvride, Lane's business partner, who represented the Lane family at the execution. Those present held their breaths. Was Blake at long last going to incriminate Robert Lane as her seducer, if not accomplice? McIlvride mounted the steps. "Do not think too hardly of me," she said, holding out her hand. "Good-bye."

"With deliberate firmness she stepped on the trap and a smile crossed her face...Her body swayed slightly after the black cap had been pulled over her head. In a couple seconds, it seemed like minutes, the form of the poor girl shot from view. A gasp escaped those around. She died without a word of regret." ◦

CHAPTER 2

DEATH OF A LADY'S MAN

BLOODY JACK KRAFCHENKO

People thought John Krafchenko could do almost anything, and so did John Krafchenko.

Everyone, from judges to lawyers to fellow crooks to girlfriends, saw in him that special something that can't be explained. Women, in particular, felt his charisma. At his execution, his stepmother believed he would come back to life even after a prison doctor pronounced him dead.

"Someone should make a movie," people often say when discussing Krafchenko, Manitoba's notorious Ukrainian bandit, because he carried out his crimes with such daring and showmanship.

In between stick-ups, bad cheques and bank holdups, Krafchenko assumed identities as a physician, a dentist, a temperance speaker, and a college teacher. He once toured the United States as a professional wrestler under aliases Tommy Ryan and Pearl Smith.

He went to jail in 1905 for paying a poker debt with a rubber cheque—to a Mountie. It was one of many bad cheques he wrote while posing as a temperance lecturer crisscrossing rural Manitoba and Saskatchewan.

Police commented on how intelligent and cultured Krafchenko was. Krafchenko would call them "boys" and tell them jokes and smile. He spoke five languages, English, Ukrainian, Romanian, German, and Russian. He dressed sharply, was well-mannered, and could hold his liquor. He was a skilled locksmith and top-notch mechanic but Harry Gray, the father of popular history writer James H. Gray, told his son he once worked with Krafchenko and he was lazy. Maybe that was part of his problem.

Women sat in the front row during his preliminary hearing in Winnipeg, definitely not a woman's place in the early 1900s.

Krafchenko was a suspect in many more robberies than he was ever charged with. In 1902, he rode a freighter across the Atlantic Ocean to escape a robbery he committed in Plum Coulee, Manitoba. He once robbed a bank in Milan, Italy, ran to his nearby hotel to change, then joined the crowd of onlookers to watch the excitement. He complained when he got back to Winnipeg how poor business was in Europe because the English and Germans weren't familiar with stick-ups, as if he had to explain it to his victims.

Krafchenko broke out of jail twice, and once escaped police custody by jumping handcuffed out a train window, only to be tracked down in a farmhouse somewhere in Saskatchewan. He mesmerized men and women alike. In one jailbreak in Winnipeg, he convinced both his lawyer and a police guard to break him out. The police guard, who'd won an award for bravery just a few years earlier, received a seven-year jail term for his complicity and died in prison.

People claim that after Krafchenko broke out of jail in Winnipeg, he strolled past the police station in midday laughing, and then walked along downtown streets smiling and nodding at passersby. That would have been like him. He had amazing bravado. Even during his murder trial he sat looking amused.

People loved him and feared him. He had a hair-trigger temper. The *Manitoba Free Press* said Krafchenko could intimidate with a look. "Witnesses…faltered in their testimony as he gazed from the prisoner's dock," the *Free Press* said. Much was always made of Krafchenko's eyes. The *Manitoba Free Press* described them as "lustrous." Winnipeg taxi driver Ben Rolph, who wrote a short book about his association with Krafchenko, said he had "eyes of steel grey."

Rolph described Krafchenko as "a man of striking appearance." He had Hollywood looks. He had prominent cheekbones, deep-set eyes and shaggy eyebrows. He looks like George Clooney in his mug shot, but Krafchenko does him one better with an adorable chin dimple. He combined those looks with a smouldering, Robert Mitchum-like insouciance.

And Krafchenko was a lady's man. Manitoba newspapers in 1914 only hinted at Krafchenko's sex appeal. Women sat in the front row during his preliminary hearing in Winnipeg, definitely not a woman's place in the early 1900s. On another occasion, the *Manitoba Free Press* reported: "Quite a large number of women were in court, an unprecedented occurrence." One female witness "was continually gazing at Krafchenko," and was told to stop by the Crown. When she didn't, the Crown asked that her status be changed to "hostile witness."

The *Winnipeg Telegram* printed an article that quoted three women expressing admiration for Krafchenko. The article ran immediately following Krafchenko's sensational escape from the Winnipeg Police Jail overnight on Jan. 10, 1914. The *Manitoba*

Free Press, on the same day, also pointed out the criminal's appeal to the fairer sex. "It is certain that the sympathy of Winnipeg women in general is with the clever criminal," the *Free Press* said. "Just why a self-confessed criminal should make so strong a personal appeal to that half of society, which is commonly supposed to stand solidly for moral uplift and law enforcement, is hard to understand."

It takes a brief pause to figure out why the newspapers were suddenly saying these things. It was a roundabout way to suggest that female admirers of Krafchenko may have helped him escape. The accusations were too much for suffragette leader Nellie McClung, then 40, whose activism would help Manitoba women win the right to vote two years later and make Manitoba the first province to do so.

"It seems like a cheap and unworthy attempt to discredit the intelligence of women as a class," McClung wrote in the Letters to the Editor. She specifically took aim at the *Telegram* article: "Of course, there are moral degenerates in all classes, high and low, rich and poor, male and female, but just why their idiotic driveling should be given space in a reputable paper, is a matter of wonder."

Another woman letter writer also took aim at the *Telegram*: "There follow three statements purporting to be made by club and newspaper women expressing ardent admiration for the desperado. Personally, I do not believe for one moment that the statements are genuine. They bear all the earmarks of a cub reporter beginning his career in the yellowest of the yellow school."

The letters ran in the *Manitoba Free Press* on Jan. 12, but not in the *Telegram*. The *Telegram* issued an apology the next day. The length of the apology is one rarely seen in newspapers. "Probably a few foolish girls may have pleasure over the escape of the murderer, but the great mass of women, as men, hark back to the woe caused by this man's crime," the newspaper said. It blamed the article "on the super-heated imagination of the young woman" who wrote the piece.

One female not charmed by Krafchenko was 11-year-old Mary Doerksen. Doerksen was a star witness at Krafchenko's murder trial. It was a classic confrontation: a child's innocence versus Krafchenko's smouldering charm; "Little Mary Doerksen," as the newspapers dubbed her, versus Bloody Jack. Other witnesses feared for their lives giving evidence against Krafchenko. Not Little Mary. She sat posture-perfect on the witness stand and spoke with a clear, scrubbed-clean voice bred of her devout Mennonite upbringing. "Do you know what will happen if you do not tell the truth?" the Crown asked the little girl. "Yes. God will punish us," she said.

In a climatic moment of Krafchenko's murder trial, her voice rang out almost in sing-song: "It was John Krafchenko," she testified. The *Manitoba Free Press* reported that Krafchenko's facial muscles tightened, but then he smiled.

CRIMES OF THE CENTURY

Krafchenko wasn't yet handsome, just rakishly cute, when he first appeared as a tyke before a Winnipeg magistrate for stealing five watches from a store where he worked.

Krafchenko wasn't yet handsome, just rakishly cute, when he first appeared as a tyke before a Winnipeg magistrate for stealing five watches from a store where he worked. 'Boy Charged with the Larceny of Five Watches', a small headline in the *Manitoba Free Press* read, and a short tongue-in-cheek account followed about how the magistrate gave the 11-year-old boy "a wholesome lecture."

John Larry Krafchenko was born in 1881 to Ukrainian parents living in Romania. They immigrated to Canada in 1888 and settled in Plum Coulee, 100 kilometers south of Winnipeg, where his father worked as a blacksmith. The son was a hellraiser from the outset. Winnipeg police historian Constable John Burchill wrote that "Krafchenko exhibited a violently aggressive streak towards authority figures." People quickly learned not to cross him, and he was impossible to discipline. He was in trouble so often that by age 15 he was incarcerated for stealing a bicycle in Morden.

"Early on he accepted the doctrine of people in his class that society, having frowned on his family and turned against him as a youth, was his enemy," the *Winnipeg Telegram* claimed. The statement referred to Krafchenko's immigrant status. To many in the immigrant class, he tweaked the noses of the upper class and was therefore a hero.

Upon his release from his first short stint in jail for stealing the bicycle, Krafchenko moved to the United States and shortly after shipped out on a steamer to Australia. There he learned to be a wrestler, returned to North America around 1900 and toured the U.S. and Canada under wrestling aliases Australian Tommy Ryan and Pearl Smith. Frank W. Anderson, author of *Outlaws of Manitoba*, maintains "Pearl Smith" was Krafchenko disguised as a lady wrestler and travelling with a circus.

By age 21, Krafchenko quit wrestling and came back to Manitoba. In late 1901, a Morden sheriff was held up at gunpoint and robbed. The thief was never caught. Krafchenko was working with a threshing team less than a mile away at the time.

In 1902, he toured the province as a temperance speaker, writing bad cheques as he went. He was sentenced to 18 months in Prince Albert Penitentiary, tried to escape on the train en route, and was recaptured. Then, while in Prince Albert and assigned to paint the prison's outside wall, he knocked a guard over the head with a paint can and escaped successfully this time.

In September of that same year, he stopped a Bank of Hamilton vehicle at gunpoint between Plum Coulee and Winkler, and made off with $2,500. He fled to New York, then worked on a large freighter bound for Europe, where he practised crime from England to Italy, including the Milan bank caper. He moved to Russia—Russian was one of the languages in which he was fluent—where he married, and the couple returned to Manitoba in 1906. He robbed Plum Coulee's Bank of Hamilton again, and fled to the U.S. He was caught back

MAYHEM ON MAIN STREET

ROBBERY

Up until 1911, Winnipeg's finest did not carry firearms. Then the Mecum brothers hit town. After a daring escape from a penitentiary in Anomosa, Iowa in which a prison guard was shot, Bert and Charles Mecum boarded a northbound train and ended up in Winnipeg. The boys immediately went on a housebreaking spree.

On August 23, a citizen reported a couple of shady looking characters lurking around Elmwood. Constable William Traynor was on his way across the Louise Bridge when he encountered the Mecum brothers. They pulled guns and fled through the Brown and Rutherford lumber yards.

Traynor followed, and after borrowing a gun from the lumber yard office, traced Bert and Charles to a house in the Rover Avenue area. Two other officers arrived, and they flushed the crooks, who came out of the house shooting. Traynor was hit, the boys took off, and Constable Hugh Brown gave chase. As they crashed through people's yards, the Mecums continued shooting at Brown, who returned "fire" by throwing stones at them.

Reaching Sutherland Avenue, Bert and Charles tried to commandeer a streetcar. The conductor, ignoring the guns in his face, refused to co-operate. So they jumped in a horse-drawn buggy, wildly blasting away. Before they could giddy up, a passer-by leapt into the fray, grabbed one of the horses, and wouldn't let go. One of the boys tried to shoot him but hit the horse, which dropped like the Dow Jones. By now, there were several bobbies at the scene, and they all piled into the buggy and pummelled the Mecum brothers into submission. While in custody, they were uncooperative until a liberal dose of police batons was applied to their persons, at which point a confession ensued.

The Mecum boys got a total of 17 years for their escapade.

The *Anomosa Eureka* reported that there was little regret that the boys would do their time north of the border, noting that "...Canadian prisons make the Iowa institutions parlors of delight."

Miraculously, Traynor was the only casualty of this Wild West shoot-out. Though he survived the shooting, he died shortly thereafter of a fever. Both Traynor and Brown were awarded the King's Police Medal; the first time in Canadian history that it was awarded for gallantry, and the Winnipeg police were promptly issued firearms.

CRIMES OF THE CENTURY

• Uniformed constables and detectives pose in front of Winnipeg's Rupert Street station.

in Manitoba when he made a surprise appearance at the trial of a friend.

His unexpected return caused the kind of sensation Krafchenko craved. He loved for people to talk about "Krafchenko." His surprise testimony helped acquit his friend but Krafchenko was sentenced to three years in Stony Mountain Penitentiary for his previous crimes. He got out in 1910 and vowed to go straight. He moved his family to Graham, Ontario, where he worked as a labourer with Grand Trunk Pacific railway. With his talent as a mechanic and machinist and with his leadership skills, he was quickly promoted to foreman. He and his wife had their first child in October, 1913.

Perhaps the frustrations of a normal life were too much for him. He was a man other criminals feared and he had the run of Winnipeg's underworld. It couldn't have been easy taking orders at the railway. Krafchenko's famous temper didn't intimidate railway managers the way it did people on the street. It was his temper that got him demoted back to labourer. So Krafchenko quit, and temporarily left his wife and newborn on the premise he was going to Manitoba to look for work. Back in Manitoba, Krafchenko went looking for the big payoff. Police records show that on Nov. 18, 1913, Krafchenko purchased six Winchester rifles, a 9 mm Browning automatic handgun, and a 7.65 Luger handgun, from the Hingston/Smith Arms Company in Winnipeg. He claimed the guns were for a hardware store he owned in Plum Coulee. The weapons were to be shipped to him there. Two weeks later he entered the Bank of Montreal in Plum Coulee and pointed the Browning automatic at bank manager Henry Medley Arnold.

It was a robbery imbued with Krafchenko's trademark bravado. It was noon hour, it was in his hometown where most everyone knew him, and Krafchenko wore a disguise. It was as if he wanted people to know it was him but not be able to prove it.

Arnold was working in the bank alone over the lunch hour, as Krafchenko knew he would be. Arnold was surprised but not afraid when Krafchenko approached, and is believed to have warned Krafchenko to abort the robbery. Krafchenko persisted, grabbed the money, about $4,200—the equivalent of $65,000 in today's dollars—and started to run. Arnold gave chase.

Krafchenko wore a black coat with the fur collar turned up, a black hat, and a fake black beard. He told his getaway driver to look for someone dressed "like an old Jew." It was a plausible disguise in Plum Coulee, which comprised one of the largest Jewish communities in western Canada outside an urban centre. About 80 Jews lived in the town of 400, and a rabbi regularly visited. The Jewish community lived among other German, Ukrainian and Mennonite immigrants, making it a very Manitoban cross-section of the wave of immigrants that followed the first Scottish and French settlers.

What Plum Coulee witnesses claimed to see was the bank manager chase after the thief in the lane behind the bank, and catch him, only to be pushed away. As Arnold tried to catch him a second time, the thief turned around and shot him through the shoulder. Arnold whirled around and landed face down in an ash heap. The ashes pancaked to his sweaty face. The bullet had glanced off Arnold's shoulder blade into the vertebrae, where it severed the spinal cord. He died soon after. The killer had dropped a packet of bills and stepped over Arnold to pick it up, before running off to the getaway car.

A province-wide manhunt ensued for Krafchenko, the number one suspect. Within a week police surrounded him at 439 College Avenue in Winnipeg, where Krafchenko was posing as a St. John's College school teacher. They also found about $2,400 buried under the fence, as well as Krafchenko's next disguise: a black skirt, black petticoat, black Persian lamb muff and ruff, black wig, black veil, and women's black gloves. Krafchenko planned to disguise himself as a woman to get out of Winnipeg.

Krafchenko wasn't finished with surprises. His preliminary hearing began in Winnipeg, and Krafchenko looked confident and amused throughout. "Get through this thing so I can go rabbit shooting in spring," he told court. The night the pre-trial wrapped up, with Krafchenko committed to stand trial for murder in Morden, he escaped again.

• Winnipeg was one of the first cities in North America to use the call box system for improved communications.

CRIMES OF THE CENTURY

Amazingly, Constable Robert Reid, one of the guards that night, and Krafchenko's lawyer Percy Hagel, the son of one of western Canada's most famous criminal lawyers, helped him escape.

Police were aware of Krafchenko's history of escapes, and thought it would be safest to hold him in the Winnipeg Police Jail as a precaution. But instead of keeping him in the cells with other prisoners, police decided to lock him in the old kitchen on the second floor. At about 2:30 a.m., Krafchenko unlocked the room with a smuggled key, walked out and pointed a revolver at the two police guards. "I'm going to get out of here, boys," he told the two policemen, waving a gun back and forth at them. He locked the guards in a closet and threw a clothesline out an unbarred window. As he was scaling the rope it broke about 40 feet from the ground. Krafchenko injured a knee and ankle in the fall, and hobbled off to a getaway car. Amazingly, Constable Robert Reid, one of the guards that night, and Krafchenko's lawyer Percy Hagel, the son of one of western Canada's most famous criminal lawyers N.F. Hogel, helped him escape. Reid would eventually receive a seven year jail term, and Hagel three years. After serving his time, Hagel was reinstated as a lawyer, something that would never happen today.

Two weeks later police again found Krafchenko in Winnipeg's north end. He had a couple of revolvers laying around his room but was caught by surprise and went quietly with police, limping from the injuries from his fall from the second storey jail. Police reported that Krafchenko was cordial and smiling as they led him away. In mid March of 1914, Krafchenko was finally brought to Morden to stand trial. Between the trial into his escape, and Krafchenko's trial for the murder of Arnold, Krafchenko's name appeared on the front page of the *Manitoba Free Press* for 32 straight days.

As the murder trial began, newspapers of the day had a bit of sport with the town's immigrant mix, when residents were called to testify. The *Manitoba Free Press* reported that no one could understand a group of Mennonite witnesses. It took three translators to decipher what was at first thought to be German, but then was simply called "speaking Mennonite." In fact, the Mennonites spoke what is called Low German, which originates from northern Germany and has similarities to the Dutch language.

Also noteworthy was the testimony of Plum Coulee Jewish merchant Sam Rosner, whose daughter Saidye would go on to marry Sam Bronfman and help launch the Bronfman financial empire. Early on in the trial, the Crown established that a "man in black" robbed the Plum Coulee bank and shot Arnold. But no one could establish the man in black's identity. Neither could Rosner, but he did confirm the man in black killed Arnold. "That fellow turned round and shoot Mr. Arnold," Rosner told court.

It never seems fair that a killer achieves a sort of immortality in history, while his victim gets a single day's write-up in the newspaper and then is forgotten. Besides the usual platitudes for a victim, the newspapers said

Arnold moved from the Maritimes 10 years earlier to work for the Bank of Montreal, first in Brandon for eight years, then Plum Coulee. He was a church-going Anglican. He had a brother who was shot fighting for the British in South Africa in the Boer War. "Mr. Arnold comes of fighting stock…It is this trait which cost him his life," the *Free Press* surmised.

The *Free Press* said Arnold "was highly respected for his manly qualities and attractive personality, and it was typical of him that he would fight an armed robber, single-handed, rather than duck behind the counter." But there is little else said of the man, other than a witness to the shooting who claimed he heard Arnold's last words while pursuing the man in black. The words are so apropos they should be enshrined on a bank manager coat of arms somewhere. "Drop that money," Arnold shouted just before he was shot. His wife and children moved away shortly after the funeral.

The Crown called over 70 witnesses. No one could identify positively that Krafchenko was the man in black. The getaway driver, the final witness, would identify that it was Krafchenko, but William Dyck could be discredited since he had a criminal record, and there were doubts that he was the naive victim he claimed to be after a packet of $100 from the same Bank of Montreal was found under his car seat.

Dyck, a taxi driver, claimed he was only told to wait for Krafchenko at a specified time to give him a ride. Dyck testified his getaway car raced at the break-neck speed of 25-35 miles per hour from Plum Coulee to Winnipeg, with Krafchenko threatening him with his gun and even firing a bullet inches from his head through the getaway car's cloth roof. Some roads were so bad that Dyck drove just five miles per hour for long stretches.

MURDER BY ACCIDENT

A farm hand took the lives of his employers in Stonewall on December 9, 1916. Bertrand John Patrick Spain, 16, shot and killed Jamie Vincent and his wife. Both were shot in the face with a rifle: Mrs. Vincent in her kitchen, Mr. Vincent in the granary. Spain testified that he shot Mrs. Vincent by accident, and shot Mr. Vincent because he feared the husband would try to exact revenge. He then took the Vincent's savings to help his getaway. Spain had a history of insanity in his family. He was sentenced to hang but Ottawa granted a stay of execution due to his age.

Who was the man in black? Mary Doerksen's role in the trial was to fill in that gap in the Crown's evidence. The newspapers were abuzz with the surprise witness, who had not been part of Krafchenko's pre-trial in Winnipeg.

"Oh yeah, mother talked about that," said Dorothy Penner, in an interview in Morden where she lives. Penner is the daughter of Mary Brown, nee Doerksen, who passed away in 1993. "She knew when she saw him in the courthouse, she knew it was him. She had no doubt about that," said Dorothy.

The Krafchenkos lived within viewing distance of Mary's house. Mary's mother sometimes took pity on Krafchenko and would

SCANDAL AT THE LEGISLATURE

FRAUD

Scandals involving politicians are nothing new. But Manitoba politicians got off to a bad start when their spanking new Legislative Building was centre of a controversy.

In the election of 1914, the Conservatives won a narrow victory over the resurgent Liberals, who privately attributed their defeat to political corruption. Rodmond P. Roblin, who had succeeded Hugh John MacDonald as premier in 1900, led the Tories. Already controversial because of his arrogant manner, Roblin had surrounded himself with a fiercely partisan political machine that put himself and the party above everything, including, as events were to prove, the law.

In 1913, the firm of Thomas Kelly and Sons was awarded the contract to build the new Legislative Assembly for the sum of $2,859,750. Shortly after the contract was signed, V.W. Horwood, the Provincial Architect, recommended changes, which upped the ante to $4,500.000. This was approved, and construction began. Almost immediately, a swirl of rumours about shoddy construction and kickbacks began circulating. The Liberals were now convinced that their electoral loss was the result of corruption. The Liberals demanded an investigation at the opening session of the legislature in 1915.

The Public Accounts Committee began looking into the matter on March 11. A.B. Hudson and T.H. Johnson ably represented the Liberals, but the deck was stacked. To begin with, a key construction inspector was not available for questioning. It was subsequently proved that a Conservative member of the Committee had advised the inspector to absent himself from the province during the inquiry. In addition, Horwood provided false testimony.

The Liberals were stymied, and the Conservatives then used their majority on the Committee to approve the contract, and thought that would be the end of it. Not so fast, cried A.B. Hudson. On March 31, he introduced a motion charging the government with fraud and culpable negligence, and calling for a Royal Commission. Nobody on the other side of the aisle blinked, and the motion was defeated. Today, this would have closed the issue. However, the Liberals had one more card to play, which was to petition the Lieutenant-Governor. In that era, the Queen's representative tended to be far more activist than would be acceptable today, and Sir Douglas Cameron issued an ultimatum to Roblin. Appoint a Royal Commission, or resign.

With no wiggle room left, Roblin appointed the Royal Commission, which commenced proceedings on April 27, and very quickly affirmed the allegations made by the Liberals. On May 12, the Roblin government resigned, and when the full story was unearthed, Roblin and four of his ministers were arrested and charged with conspiracy to defraud the government. Their trial began on July 24, 1916, and when the jury was unable to reach a verdict, a new trial was ordered. Eventually, all charges were dropped due to the ill-health of two of the accused, including Roblin, although it must be noted that Roblin lived another twenty years.

Meanwhile, an action was brought against Thomas Kelly, which resulted in a conviction, a sentence of two years, and an order of restitution in the amount of $1,207,351.65. Only $30,000 was ever recovered, and the province carried the balance on its books until 1941. Personally disgraced, Roblin died in 1937 at Hot Springs, Arkansas. It would be left to his grandson Duff to restore the lustre to the Roblin name.

• Rodmon P. Roblin

have him in their house to eat. "Krafchenko had very dark eyes and my mother didn't like the looks of him. She didn't like it when he looked at you," said Dorothy.

In Plum Coulee three weeks before the robbery, Krafchenko had chased little Mary around a table in the Commercial Hotel in Plum Coulee, pretending that he was trying to get a kiss from the little girl. Mary ran home frightened.

"Did he kiss you?" the Crown asked. "No, because he did not catch me," Mary replied.

When taking the stand, Mary told court she could not swear on the bible. Why? the Crown asked. "Because our religion don't let us swear," she replied.

Mary testified that on the day of the robbery-murder, she passed within five feet of the disguised Krafchenko while on her way home from school to have lunch.

"Mary Doerksen spoke distinctly in her pleasant, child voice, the words, 'It was John Krafchenko,'" the *Free Press* reported. How did she know it was him, if he wore a disguise, she was asked. "By his eyes," she replied.

Krafchenko's lawyer scoffed that a child could identify Krafchenko by his eyes, but the Crown turned the argument around, suggesting the jury look at Krafchenko. He asked if anyone could forget those eyes.

There was always public fascination with Krafchenko. Throughout the trial, he was confident, cheerful, smiling, and sometimes

Mary testified that on the day of the robbery-murder, she passed within five feet of the disguised Krafchenko while on her way home from school to have lunch.

CRIMES OF THE CENTURY

"He devoted numerous looks to the ladies seated in the grand jury box, and appreciated their smiles at his sallies."

laughing. He boasted that he would never be convicted. The daily news reports were constantly updating Krafchenko's demeanor. For example, at the trial of his co-conspirators who helped spring him from jail, a trial which directly preceded his own murder trial, the *Manitoba Free Press* said of Krafchenko: "Never in the least perturbed, he appeared to be playing to the gallery all the time. His snappy and amusing answers came out during cross-examination." It continued: "He devoted numerous looks to the ladies seated in the grand jury box, and appreciated their smiles at his sallies."

The public's fascination intensified during his murder trial. From the *Manitoba Free Press:* Mar. 25— "Krafchenko was very pale this morning. He smiled now and then in his bright way but on the whole his attitude is alert and strained...There is a kind of tigerish intensity about him." Mar. 30— "Outwardly carefree and debonair, the prisoner nevertheless reveals to a close observer some signs of strain." Apr. 2— "The prisoner is still cheerful most of the time. He seems debonair and carefree at times, and then again there are some moments when he appears keenly anxious." Apr. 8— "Sometimes today the prisoner's face seemed to show signs of nervousness...Then in a few minutes, he would appear more casual and unconcerned than any other person in the room. He would stretch himself, and settling down placidly, chew tobacco, using freely a spittoon which had been provided for him."

No wonder Krafchenko's confidence was beginning to wane. The jury returned a guilty verdict. Krafchenko was sentenced to hang. He showed little expression. The *Manitoba Free Press* tracked down Krafchenko's father Eli living in a Transcona boarding house at the corner of Pandora Avenue and Bond Street. "Ugh!" was the father's tortured response when told the verdict by the reporter.

"Bloody Jack" Krafchenko was tremendously popular, especially among the lower class immigrants. Even in Plum Coulee, he had supporters who hoped he would beat the charges. "He was an excellent liar and a most persuasive man," said Rolph, who taxied Krafchenko around for several days prior to the bank robbery and later published an account of it. Rolph said Krafchenko had a way with people, "a quiet smile that took the embarrassment out of a situation."

A letter to Krafchenko's wife was produced during the trial. "Accept my love and be healthy," he wrote to his wife Fanica, who waited faithfully for him in Graham, Ontario. Krafchenko sent along $500. The letter was written in Romanian and translated for the trial.

But witnesses gave other accounts of Krafchenko. A hotel clerk testified that Krafchenko, using one of his aliases, checked into a Winnipeg hotel with another woman he claimed was his wife. The usually unflappable Krafchenko blushed during the testimony.

There has always been speculation that Krafchenko was well acquainted with women associated with Winnipeg's underworld including women of the night. While there is no definitive proof, it is conjectured that Krafchenko knew these working women more than just casually, and they may have made up some of his supporters in the courtroom.

A second love letter allegedly surfaced after the trial. This time Krafchenko wrote a 17-year-old girl living near Plum Coulee, according to Ben Bertram, or Ben Abramovich as he was known in Plum Coulee before he moved away and changed his name. A member of the town's Jewish community, Bertram self-published an autobiography before passing away several years ago. Bertram said he and his sister Rose saw the shooting that day but were kept out of the trial because of their young ages.

Before the murder, Bertram said Krafchenko returned to Plum Coulee after losing his job in fall of 1913, and got some work from an area farmer. People let bygones be bygones and Krafchenko was welcomed back into the community. People wanted to believe Krafchenko was reformed. Bertram maintains Krafchenko attended church and made friends with people. However, while under the employ of the area farmer, he was caught getting amorous with the farmer's 17-year-old daughter. The farmer chased him off.

Bertram claims Krafchenko wrote the 17-year-old girl while he awaited execution. In the letter, he professed his love for her. The reason Bertram knew about the letter was it was written in Romanian and the girl brought it to his parents to translate. Bertram's parents were from Romania originally and the only ones in the area who could translate it. "(Krafchenko) begged forgiveness of the Arnold family, swearing he had warned Mr. Arnold he would have to shoot if followed. He had not intended to kill," the letter said. The Abramovich family later moved to California. Excerpts from Bertram's autobiography are contained in the *Plum Coulee Centennial Book, 1901-2001*.

It's hard to determine how much of Bertram's account can be believed. It likely contains some grains of truth, but which grains? It seems a story told to him by his parents, which may have been modified for a child's understanding, and in turn modified somewhat romantically by Bertram's memory. Bertram's sympathy is typical of how many people felt about Krafchenko.

Many people tried to help Krafchenko. One judge offered to personally assist Krafchenko get a job. Winnipeg Chief of Police Donald MacPherson once paid him money up front to help him find out who was responsible for a series of safe blowings in Manitoba. Krafchenko took the money and never reported back. There are numerous accounts in Plum Coulee of local people trying to assist Krafchenko, including merchant Sam Rosner. Plum Coulee barber John Reichert claimed he advised Krafchenko to go straight the day

On his last night, Krafchenko stayed up until 4 a.m. before collapsing. Reverend Berthal Heeney stayed with him through the night.

before the robbery, when Krafchenko came into his shop for a shave.

Prior to the robbery, Krafchenko went around town boasting he wanted to hold up the Plum Coulee bank, it was revealed at his trial. Which was another thing about Krafchenko. He was a common braggart. He spoke freely and loudly so anyone could hear. He wanted people to hear what he did and what he would do. Which may have explained his penchant for sensational robberies and escapes. He liked people talking about him.

In the days leading up to Krafchenko's execution, Manitoba Chief Justice Howell received a letter written in blood threatening all those connected with the Krafchenko case. A petition reputed to contain 20,000 names and weighing 12 pounds pleading for clemency was submitted to Ottawa but rejected.

The night before he was to hang, the *Free Press* reported that a crowd of 300 gathered outside his "death cell," in the Vaughan Street Jail, "the greater part of which were women." The reporter said the crowd's objective "was the hope of catching a glimpse of the condemned man as the light made plain the interior of the cell from the ceiling down to a couple feet of wall." Executions were carried out in the Vaughan Street Jail yard, and Krafchenko would have heard the lumber being sawed and hammered up to that fateful day.

"Krafchenko is bearing up badly...Last night he scarcely slept at all and eats practically nothing. He is now a physical wreck of himself," the *Free Press* said days before.

On his last night, Krafchenko stayed up until 4 a.m. before collapsing. Reverend Berthal Heeney stayed with him through the night. "Krafchenko's last conversations were punctuated with tears and sobs for his wife and boy, and genuine penitence," according to the minister. The minister showed a pewter spoon, the handle of which was scarred and bent as if by prying. "Krafchenko lifted the lock of his cell door in my presence last night," Heeney said, fueling the legend that Krafchenko could have escaped again if he wanted. "You can tell the papers I have more nerve than ever," Krafchenko told Heeney. Krafchenko was always trying to spin the papers.

Ten minutes before the execution, Krafchenko was revived and given morphine to steady his nerves. He was held as he climbed the scaffold. "He gave his head a shake to get the wisps of long hair out of his eyes," before the black cap was placed over his head, the *Free Press* reported. The hangman pulled the trap.

Krafchenko is buried in the Brookside Cemetery in an unmarked grave, in Lot 546, section 22.

THE GALS IN BLUE

PERSONNEL

It's no secret that in the early years of the 20th century Winnipeg was a hard living town. Saloons were everywhere, and prostitution was rampant, which resulted in a wide variety of social as well as legal problems. Orphaned or neglected children required special care, and of course dealing with the ladies of the night was always a delicate matter for an all-male police force.

Accordingly, the Winnipeg Police Commission, on December 22, 1916, authorized the appointment of two female constables. Just five days later Mary Dunn was hired, becoming not only Winnipeg's first policewoman, but also one of the first in Canada. A week later, Mary was joined on the force by Jane Andrews. Both women were in their early 40's, and were attached to the Morality Division where they functioned more as matrons than peace officers. Their only equipment was a badge and a whistle, and on the rare occasions that they left the police station, male officers always escorted them.

Mary Dunn left the force in 1920, and she was replaced by Clara Donaldson, also in her early forties. There were no further female additions to the force until 1941, when Clara retired. Her replacement, Helen Hansford, ushered in the modern era for female officers in that she ventured out onto the mean streets by herself. Jane Andrews retired in 1938, and Hansford was the only female officer on the force for 19 years.

By 1957, mixed beverage rooms had been sanctioned, and the force promoted two women from matron to policewoman, and hired a third. It was also in 1957 that policewomen were armed for the first time, but only with "blackjacks."

Prior to the 1970s, female officers were not accorded the same status as the men. They were paid less for the same work, and there was almost no opportunity for advancement. This changed with amalgamation in 1974. Training was standardized, the women went on patrol, and they got pay equity. Promotion remained a thorny issue, however, and it was not until 1995 that Shelly Hart became the first woman to achieve the rank of Inspector.

Today, female officers are a common sight, although the force does not deploy female-only squad cars.

• Mary Dunn

CHAPTER 3

BOOZE, GLORIOUS BOOZE!
BILL WOLCHOCK AND PROHIBITION IN MANITOBA

A pair of employees talking on the floor of the CNR shops in Transcona sounds like an unlikely launch to the biggest bootleg operation in Manitoba history.

It was the early 1920s under Prohibition. Leonard Wolchock, 74, son bootlegger Bill Wolchock, tells the story.

"Sonny (nickname), a CNR boilermaker, one day came up to my dad, who was a machinist with the railway, and asked if he could make a part for him. 'What's it for?' my dad asked. 'It's for a still,' Sonny said. Sonny was making stills for farmers out in the country. My dad said, 'Sonny, you want to make a still? I'll make you a still and we're not going to fool around!'"

What began as a still to make a little booze for themselves and friends during Canada's Prohibition, soon turned into something much bigger. The two CNR workers realized there was an insatiable thirst for their product. "I don't think dad planned to be in the business for a long time. It just was going good," said Leonard.

"Before you know it, my dad was making big booze. He could knock out almost 1,000 gallons a day. He wasn't one of these Mickey Mouse guys making 10 gallons like in the country, like in Libau and all these places. And as time went by, he became very big." Sonny and Wolchock parted ways when Wolchock quit the railway to work full time at alcohol production, but other partners came on side. Every one of them was the same: blue collar men like Wolchock who made a living with their hands.

At the height of the Great Depression, Leonard estimates his father employed as many as 50 people who would not have been able to put food on the table otherwise.

During Prohibition in the 1920s, Bill Wolchock ran the biggest bootlegging business in Manitoba. He was producing tens of thousands of gallons of 65 per cent overproof alcohol—94 per cent pure alcohol.

Later, after his business took off, Wolchock shipped almost exclusively to the United States, and mostly to gangsters. He stored illegal alcohol in farmers' barns from the village of Reston in southwestern Manitoba, to the village of Tolstoi in southeastern Manitoba. He stored illegal booze in a coal yard that used to be on Osborne Street in Winnipeg; in a large automobile service station in St. Boniface; and in a St. Boniface lumberyard. He stored booze in a Pritchard Avenue horse barn. Those are just some of the known locations.

At the height of the Great Depression, Leonard estimates his father employed as many as 50 people who would not have been able to put food on the table otherwise. "They all had families, they all had houses, they all could put groceries on the table," thanks to the illegal liquor business, said Leonard.

Crooks or entrepreneurs?

Wolchock's story has eluded historians all these years. When Wolchock was finally caught and sentenced to five years in prison for income tax evasion, the Second World War was on and his case didn't get the publicity it might have otherwise. Besides, the Prohibition era had been over for more than a decade and was old news. Wolchock hadn't gone straight like the whiskey-making Bronfman family, but had continued to bootleg long after Prohibition ended.

Leonard Wolchock told the story of his father and a gang of North End bootleggers for the first time for this book. The story was checked against news clippings for the period.

Wolchock owned at least two large stills in Winnipeg: a huge four-story still operation in a building that was in the 1000-block on Logan Avenue, just east of McPhillips Avenue, that produced up to 400 gallons a day; and a huge still in a building that used to be on Tache Avenue, about 300 metres west of the Provencher Bridge on the river side. He also had smaller stills, often in rural locations, and owned portable stills he moved around from barn to barn outside Winnipeg to elude police.

Wolchock never considered what he was doing wrong, said his son. He thought the governments were wrong. People were going to find a way to drink one way or another.

"My father was a manufacturer. He was filling a niche market. I'm not ashamed of anything he did," said Leonard.

Even the police chief, who lived just five doors down from the Wolchock home at 409 Boyd Avenue, would drop in regularly for a friendly drink. The fire commissioner, who lived one street over on College Avenue and three houses down, was another thirsty visitor. Granted, Wolchock ran a little import liquor business as a front, which was legal at the time, but Leonard has little doubt the authorities knew what his father's main source of income was.

"The chief of police knew what my father was doing! And the fire chief was over at our place all the time!" said Leonard.

When the RCMP finally moved in on his father for income tax evasion, it was a measure of their respect for Wolchock that he was never arrested. Police called his dad with the news, said Leonard. "The police chief phoned up and said, 'Bill, I want you to come down.' They never sent anyone to get him."

Booze, glorious booze! Was it more glamorous in Prohibition when it was illegal? Or was the illegal liquor trade more harmful by turning otherwise law-abiding men into criminals? Was illegal liquor more dangerous to your health (alcohol poisoning), and did concealed drinking lead to more serious drinking problems?

While both Canada and the United States brought in Prohibition, there was a great gulf in how Prohibition played out in the two countries. Like a typical Canadian TV drama, Prohibition was more shouting than shooting in Canada. In the States, it was more shooting. Much more.

Corpses in the gangster booze wars in the U.S. were rarely found with just one or two

• Bill Wolchock and his wife taking a stroll while visiting U.S.

KEYSTONE'S COPS

PERSONNEL

It is generally believed that the first police force in the keystone province of Manitoba was the North-West Mounted Police. Not so. For more than 60 years, Manitoba had its own provincial police. Brought into existence in 1871, the Mounted Constabulary Force was headed up by Frank Villiers, who had come to Red River with the Wolseley expedition. In 1905, a special unit called the Manitoba Mounted Police was formed to combat gangs of horse thieves along the U.S. border. In 1920, the force was reorganized, and took the name of the Manitoba Provincial Police.

Initially headquartered on Lombard in Winnipeg, the force eventually moved to a Main Street location, which also housed the jail and the courthouse. Chief Villiers hired 24 men, who were paid between $20 to $30 per month. By 1874, Winnipeg had established the city police, and the provincial force was reduced to one man, Richard Power, the third chief. Power served until 1880 when he and a prisoner drowned while crossing the Red River from St. Boniface.

Much of the early activity of the force was centred on controlling the illicit liquor trade, and with the coming of Prohibition in the twenties, the force was reorganized and expanded. The provincial police were responsible for enforcing the Temperance Act, and these duties led to one of the blackest days in the force's history.

At approximately 1 a.m. on November 11, 1920, four MPP morality officers went to the Stockyards Hotel in St. Boniface. As the penalties for offences under the act were fines only, the officers were not armed. While checking hotel rooms, Constables Alex McCurdy, and James Uttley were both shot by James Buller, a well-known criminal. McCurdy died later that morning, and Uttley five days later. Buller was eventually shot dead by Chicago police.

The Manitoba Provincial Police force served until 1932, when the 74-member force was absorbed into the RCMP. Much of the history of these pioneers in policing has been lost, but their contribution to the province is not forgotten.

35

bullets in them, but four, five, eight. Gangsters adopted the submachine gun invented by John Thompson in the 1920s, variously dubbed the Tommy Gun, Chopper, Gat, and Chicago Typewriter. Frank Gusenberg took 22 bullets in the famous St. Valentine's Day Massacre in Chicago, when Al Capone's men, disguised as police officers, lined up seven of George "Bugs" Moran's men against a warehouse wall and opened fire. One creative reporter at the time wrote the machine guns "belched death."

These two news stories from a single September day in 1930 on the front page of the *Manitoba Free Press* are typical:

Detroit, Michigan: "An unidentified man was killed tonight by two assassins armed with sawed-off shotguns who stepped out of an automobile, fired four charges into the body of their victim, and escaped in the auto. It was the third gang killing of the week here.

Elizabeth, New Jersey: "Twelve gunmen waited in ambush within Sunrise Brewery here today, disarmed a raiding party of seven dry agents and shot and killed one of the invaders." One federal agent was found shot eight times. "The gangsters, who apparently had been forewarned of the raid, then escaped."

There are likely several reasons why Canada didn't go the gangster route. One, there were more loopholes in Canadian law to get liquor if you wanted. For example, you could get a prescription for "medical" brandy. Two, we have never been as gun-happy as the Americans. And three, our Prohibition didn't last as long. Prohibition in the U.S. ran from 1920-33. In Manitoba, Prohibition started in 1916 and ended in 1923.

While Canada didn't have the gang wars like down south, it did become the feeder system, the exporter, the good neighbour and free trader to the U.S. for liquor. Our Prohibition was winding down just as American Prohibition was getting started in 1920. How fortuitous for an enterprising bootlegger! Manitobans could legally buy liquor from the government and run it across the border into the hands of thirsty Americans.

And being neighbourly, we did. One of the major gateways was the Turtle Mountains in southwestern Manitoba. Booze poured through the hills, said James Ritchie, archivist with the Boissevain and Morton Regional Library.

"A long-standing tradition of smuggling through the Turtle Mountains already existed before Prohibition. People had already been smuggling things across for 50 years or more, so alcohol was just one more item of trade," Ritchie said.

Minot, Noth Dakota of all places, was a gangster haven and was dubbed "Little Chicago" back then. A railway town, it served as a distribution hub for liquor coming in from Manitoba and Saskatchewan.

While Canada didn't have the gang wars like down south, it did become the feeder system, the exporter, the good neighbour and free trader to the U.S. for liquor.

CRIMES OF THE CENTURY

When government turned off the tap, Manitobans went underground. Private stills sprang up everywhere.

The 65-kilometer border of Turtle Mountain hills are carved with trails every few kilometres so there was no way a border patrol could close down the rumrunning, said Ritchie. Many of the trails were simply road allowances where a road hadn't got built. "If you tried to across anywhere near Emerson where it's so flat, the custom guard could see you're car coming from 10 miles away. You can't do that in the Turtles. The custom guard can't see you from 500 feet away," said Ritchie.

Many a poor, southwestern Manitoba farm family augmented their income with a little rumrunning. They could buy a dozen bottles every two weeks, the government-set allotment for personal use, and sell it for profit just a few miles away. "Prohibition created an economic opportunity for a lot of families," said Ritchie.

But it was small trade compared to what the Bronfmans would do. Ekiel and Mindel Bronfman arrived in Brandon in the late 1800s. The 1901 Canada Census lists them as residents of Brandon, along with their children including Harry and Sam. It was after the Bronfmans had moved to Saskatchewan that they began selling whiskey to the United States in the 1920s. They exported whiskey by the boxcar-load. They later moved to Brandon briefly, where they continued the rumrunning, before finally setting up in Montreal.

Meanwhile, Winnipeg was the bacchanalia of the West prior to Prohibition, as the late popular history writer James H. Gray liked to say. By 1882, Winnipeg had 86 hotels, most of which had saloons. It also had five breweries, 24 wine and liquor stores, (15 of which were on Main Street), and 64 grocery stores selling whiskey. The population was just 16,000.

When government turned off the tap, Manitobans went underground. Private stills sprang up everywhere. Ukrainian farmers were famous for their stills and acted as engineering consultants for the rest of the community. The Ukrainians seemed to have an inborn talent for erecting the contraptions, and some stills made the old country potato whiskey. In Ukrainian settlements like Vita, Sundown and Tolstoi, someone's child was always assigned the task of changing the pail from under the spigot that caught the slow-dripping distilled whiskey.

Even Winnipeg Mayor Ralph Webb, who had an artificial leg and was manager of the Marlborough Hotel, campaigned for more liberal liquor laws. Webb wanted to attract tourism by promoting Winnipeg as "the city of snowballs and highballs."

The United States was interested in the Canadian experiment with Prohibition and summoned Francis William Russell, president of the Moderation League of Manitoba, a group that opposed Prohibition, to a U.S. Senate committee in Washington in 1926. Russell said Prohibition simply resulted in the proliferation of stills in Manitoba. Arrests for illegal stills rose from 40 in 1918, two years into Prohibition in Manitoba, to 300 by 1923. "We found that the province of Manitoba was covered with stills," he said. He claimed

Prohibition hadn't stopped drinking, it had just kicked it out of the public bar and into the home where it wreaked havoc on families.

One of the strangest still stories took place in the RM of Springfield just east of Winnipeg when an RCMP officer and a Customs Inspector came across a "mystery" shack. Sure enough they found a still inside and went in and began dismantling the evidence. Unknown to them, the owners arrived, saw what was going on, and set fire to the shack with them in it. The agents escaped the flames in time, but so did the arsonists, and no charges were laid.

Yet historical accounts only mention small stills in Manitoba. Some historians concluded there was no major bootlegging out of Winnipeg, just small neighbourhood and homestead stills. The story of Bill Wolchock shows that not to be true.

Winnipeg had two large thirsty markets in its vicinity: the Twin Cities, St. Paul and Minneapolis, in Minnesota, and, to a lesser extent, Chicago, Illinois.

St. Paul was a nest of gangsters. John Dillinger, Baby Face Nelson, Machine Gun Kelly, and Ma Barker and her sons, all took refuge in the city at one time or another. The person who ran the underworld in St. Paul was gangster Isadore "Kid Cann" Blumenfeld.

Chicago, of course, was the gangster capital of North America, controlled by Al Capone.

Capone was just 25 years old when he controlled Chicago. It does seem that Prohibition brought many young people into crime. Another Chicago bootlegger Hymie Weiss was gunned down by Capone's men at the tender age of 28. (Hymie Weiss was not Jewish as his name suggests but Catholic. His real name was Wajciechowski, and Hymie was a nickname.) Wolchock and his partners were in their early 20s when they started selling booze.

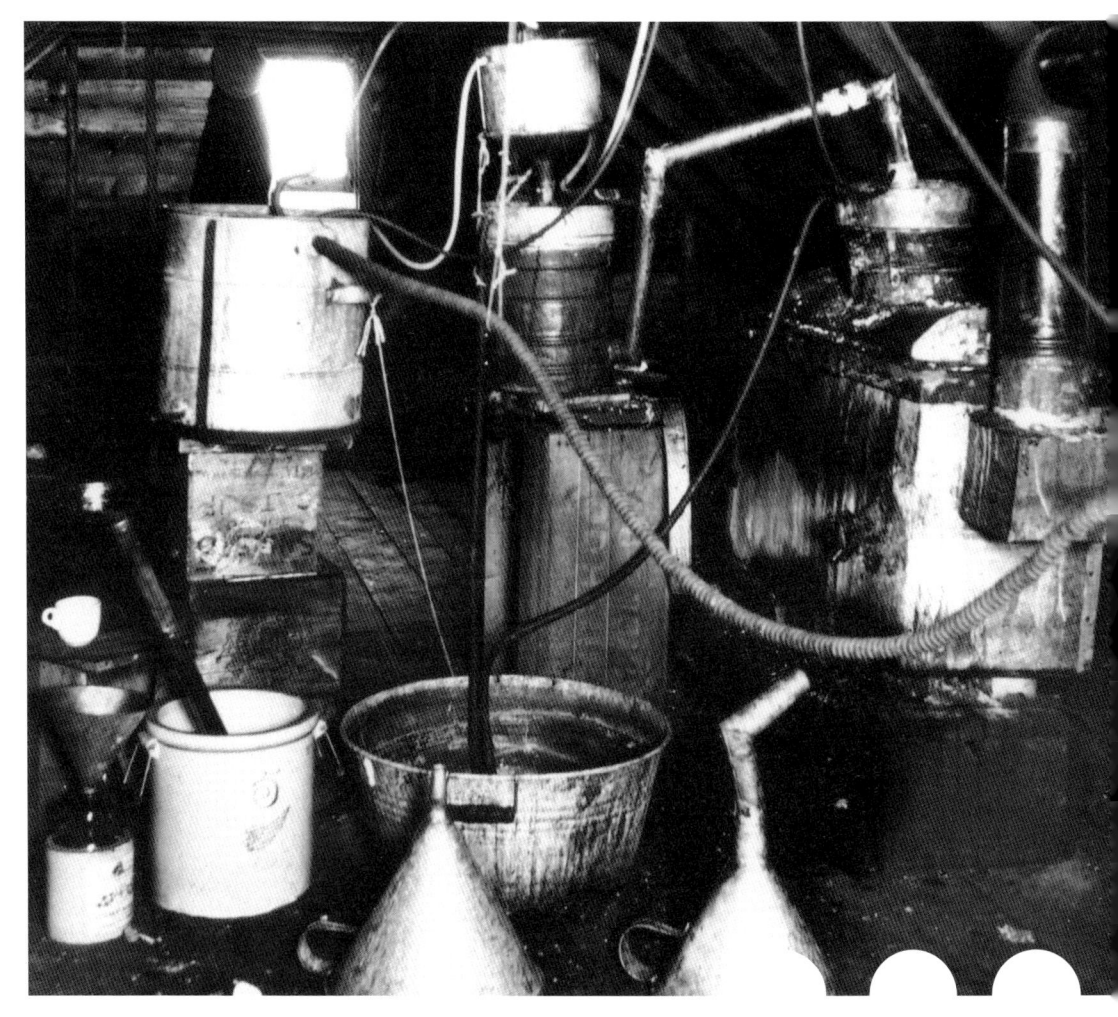

• A rudimentary still operation.

CRIMES OF THE CENTURY

• Criminals often preyed on criminals during Prohibition, by stealing proceeds from bootlegging.

Wolchock shipped pure alcohol to both the Twin Cities and Chicago, but more so to Minnesota. When his son Leonard attended a convention in Minneapolis years later, he was feted by a gangster-looking character who recognized Leonard's resemblance to his father. The gangster offered to foot his bill. Wolchock Sr. also sold to Duluth, Minnesota, and to Alberta Distilleries. It's also likely he was also shipping to Minot, since he was storing alcohol in barns in southwestern Manitoba. His business was selling to other manufacturers who brewed the pure alcohol into liquor. He would get rich from it.

Archibald William Wolchock was born in Minsk, Russia, which is now the Ukraine, in 1898, and came to Winnipeg in 1906 with his parents. He grew up and married and lived at 409 Boyd Avenue, at the corner of Boyd and Salter Street. Wolchock wasn't a gangster but he sold to them. Leonard believes his father likely dealt with Kid Cann in the Twin Cities, who ran the illegal liquor business there. "My dad did a lot of business in St. Paul," said Leonard.

Most of what Leonard knows about his dad's business was told to him by friends and associates of his dad. His father followed the code of the day and kept his business and home separate. Wolchock had a simple rule for his son if people should ask about his work: he would press his index finger to his lips.

While at Assiniboia Downs a man once approached Leonard and said he knew his dad. This sort of thing happened a lot in Leonard's life because he resembled his dad.

"The guy was a railroader," Leonard related. "He said, 'I knew your dad. We stole a train for him once. I said, 'Get out of here.' He said, 'Listen, you're dad said he had a big shipment going to Chicago that he couldn't deliver by car. I told him, Don't worry, Bill.'" The man said a crew of four, including a brakeman, pulled an engine and three boxcars over at Bergen cut-off and loaded them with alcohol. The alcohol, when it went by rail, was shipped in 45 gallon drums. Somewhere along the track the railway men switched the cars over to the Soo Line track that went to Chicago. When the payoff came, Wolchock showed up at a secret location and dished out $100 bills like playing cards to the railroaders.

The Bronfman family knew about Wolchock and Wolchock, of course, knew about them. Wolchock was friendly with the Bronfman brother-in-law Paul Matoff who ran Bronfman stores in Carduff, Gainsborough, and Bienfait, Saskatchewan, where he sold whiskey to American rumrunners. On Oct. 4, 1922, Matoff took payment from a North Dakota bootlegger. Shortly after, a 12-gauge shotgun blast killed him instantly in the railway station. The murder was never solved.

"Matoff told my dad, 'Bill, your market is in the States,'" said Leonard.

Another time a friend of Wolchock Sr. nicknamed Tubby took Leonard aside. They bumped into each other at the hospital, where Wolchock was dying. "Tubby said he and his brother had a truck and one day my dad called and asked if they had a tarp for the truck. They said yeah, so dad said, 'Go to such-and-such a place, back up your truck, don't get out, don't look in the mirror, don't do nothing. Someone will put something in your truck. Then go to this address and do the same. Don't get out, don't look in your rearview mirror, don't do nothing.' That's how business was done."

Wolchock was always a sharp dresser and wore suits and long overcoats. His shirts were specially made by Maurice Rothschild's in Minneapolis, and monogrammed AWW across the pocket. His suits were made in the Abe Palay tailor shop that used to be on Garry Street across from the old Garrick Theatre. "My dad wore a fedora because he was bald," said Leonard. One of Wolchock's favourite hangouts was the Russian Steam Baths on Dufferin Avenue, where he went Wednesdays and Saturdays. When that closed, he and his bootleg pals went to Obee's Steam Baths on McGregor near Pritchard.

Wolchock had a chain of people with various trades and skills on the payroll and always paid well. For example, he had agreements with several tinsmiths to make him the gallon cans to put the alcohol in, when it was being smuggled by car. One tinsmith told Leonard he used to make $200-$400 per week moonlighting for his father. He earned $30 a week on his day job as tinsmith.

The gallon cans would be put in jute bags and tossed in the back of a car. The drivers would go across the border at small town points like Tolstoi and Gretna. Border security back then wasn't like it is today.

Wolchock couldn't buy anything in bulk, like the sugar to make the alcohol or the cans to put the liquor into, because it would attract too much attention. So he had deals all over the place. He had a deal with a major local bakery, which used to have a central bakery and stores around Winnipeg, to supply him the sugar. He also had a deal with a bakery out on the West Coast.

Wolchock even had deals with hog farmers to get rid of the mash from alcohol production, which makes an excellent feedstuff for livestock. He had drivers and sales agents. He had a chemist on the payroll.

Wolchock also had two or three henchman. They carried guns in shoulder holsters and hung around the family but they were the only business associates that ever came to the house. "My dad lived a normal life. We sat and listened to hockey games. But he had strong-armed men around if there was any trouble," Leonard recalled.

"My dad wasn't a run-around," said Leonard. "He was a family man. He was home for lunch and dinner all the time."

Wolchock also had a friend highly placed with the federal excise office in Winnipeg. His name cannot be revealed here. He also had a high-ranking local bank official who helped him but Leonard also doesn't know in what way. Wolchock once gave his sister $30,000 to deposit in a bank, but that's all Leonard knows about the transaction. Later in life, Leonard once asked the banker, a big gruff man who always smoked a cigar, what his arrangement was with his father. "None of your f-g business," the banker snapped.

One of the problems for Wolchock was where to put the money. He made piles of money but couldn't deposit it in the bank like everyone else because he couldn't explain to authorities how he made it. Leonard thinks he stashed it, but doesn't know where. While the family didn't live ostentatiously, perhaps because that would have attracted attention, they always had money at a time when most people didn't. "People were dirt poor. There was no money around," said Leonard. All four of Wolchock's sons received vehicles when they were old enough to drive, and all would later get houses when they left home.

One of Wolchock's hobbies was collecting racehorses with names like Dark Wonder, Sun Trysts, Let's Pretend. "My dad had a stable of horses in the early days to just get rid of the money," said Leonard. Leonard's mother Rose used to travel to watch the horses race at major racetracks, like Bay Meadows in California and Hastings Park in Vancouver. Other enterprises Wolchock invested in included buying a lady's garment factory and the Sylvia Hotel in Vancouver. Leonard believes his father may have been a millionaire by the time he married Rose in 1927. Leonard was born the next year. "My mother's family was poor. Dad gave them lots of money. He paid for everything. Money was of no consequence."

His parents regularly took vacations in Hot Springs, Arkansas, which was a sort of racketeer tourist destination at the time, with

Wolchock also had two or three henchman. They carried guns in shoulder holsters and hung around the family but they were the only business associates that ever came to the house.

THE BIG SCORE

ROBBERY

Ever since Robin Hood, the public has been fascinated with hold-ups, particularly when the victim is a corporate entity, no one is seriously hurt, and the robbers make a clean getaway.

More than 75 years ago, just such a hold-up occurred in broad daylight in downtown Winnipeg. On August 14, 1925, two employees of the Winnipeg Electric Street Railway Company picked up the company payroll at the main branch of the Bank of Montreal. In those days, workers were paid in cash, and this procedure was performed twice a month. The money was then conveyed by a chauffeur driven vehicle to the Electric Railway Chambers on Notre Dame Avenue. Just inside the door, employee Robert Shaw had a gun put to his head, and was told to hand over the bag of money he was carrying. Meanwhile, two accomplices had commandeered the company car at gunpoint. The three robbers forced the chauffeur, Sid Knowler, to drive a short distance, then ordered him out of the car, and sped away.

Later that day, a patrol constable found the car near Ellice and Balmoral. The caretaker of a nearby apartment block told police she saw three men leaving the car, and was quite certain they were not carrying a bag. Another witness reported seeing another car at the scene following the getaway vehicle. Police concluded that the money had been transferred to this second vehicle.

An intensive manhunt and investigation ensued, but despite the fact that the thieves had not used disguises, police were unable to pin the crime on any of the usual suspects. The bad guys simply vanished. Their haul was a whopping $87,478.

The police eventually came to believe that the robbery was the work of American professionals, and unless a descendant fesses up, it remains as the largest unsolved robbery in the history of Winnipeg.

• The Electric Railway Building.

legal gambling introduced thanks to gangster Meyer Lansky. It also had bath houses with natural hot springs. For some reason, racketeers had a thing for steam baths and hot springs.

Leonard claims—and insists it's true—that his father would carry around $15,000 on him all the time. He once walked into a car dealership on Portage Avenue where McNaught Motors is now and bought a Cadillac on the spot with cash. "I never saw my dad with a wallet. All he had was a roll of bills with an elastic around it."

Everything was in cash. For his bootlegging business, Wolchock would buy six-to-eight cars at a time for his rumrunners to transport booze. He bought the cars at two Winnipeg dealerships where he had business relations. The first thing he always did with the new cars was tear out the back seat so he could fit in more alcohol. The stable of cars were parked inside a St. Boniface service garage where the runners had access day and night, mostly night. They sometimes went all the way to destinations like St. Paul, but usually they would just cross the border and unload into a shuttle car driven by an American rumrunner.

Wolchock and his merry men were a cross-section of Manitoba nationalities and religious origins in the 1920s. Wolchock was Jewish, and his cohorts were a mix of Poles, French, Scots, Ukrainians, Jews, Mennonite farmers near Steinbach, and Belgians, "a lot of Belgians," Leonard said.

Leonard doesn't know exactly how many people it took to run a still, maybe eight for the larger ones. When RCMP busted Wolchock's large still on Logan Avenue in 1936, it was the largest still ever found in Manitoba. Its operations extended to all four floors and into the basement, according to the *Manitoba Free Press*. The building also had an office, two vehicles, and living quarters on the third floor. Employees gained entrance to the living quarters through a crawlspace. In the living quarters were bunk beds and cooking equipment and books. The building was empty when police raided it. No charges were laid. The building was owned by the city from a tax sale.

Even after Prohibition ended and liquor was legal, it was government-controlled in Canada so good money could still be made in bootlegging. The Bronfmans had managed the tricky changeover from illegal bootlegger to legal distiller, but not Wolchock. Like most lawbreakers, he didn't quit while he was ahead.

RCMP finally charged Wolchock after customer Howard Gimble of Minneapolis got caught and ratted on him. Gimble was the key witness against Wolchock. The *Manitoba Free Press* reported that RCMP had been trying to nail Wolchock for years before Gimble gave them their break.

The charge was conspiring to defraud the federal government out of income tax moneys on liquor sales. The RCMP claimed

---

Wolchock Case Goes To Jury; Police Praised

AFTER 12 days of hearing, Chief Justice McPherson, at 12.45 p.m., gave to the assizes jury the case against William Wolchock and seven others charged with conspiracy to defraud the Dominion government of $125,000 through the operation of a still seized at Prairie Grove, Man., April 23, 1938. His Lordship spoke to the jury without interruption for two hours and 45 minutes, then adjourned court until 2.30 p.m.

he'd defrauded the government of $125,000, but that was just a figure plucked out of the air, based on the scale of operation from a single portable still. The jury was locked up for the 10-day trial because of previous suspicions of jury tampering. Gimble told court Wolchock had a portable still he moved from farm to farm near Winnipeg. RCMP found the still on Paul Demark's farm in Prairie Grove, now a bedroom community at the end of Ste. Anne's Road just past the Winnipeg perimeter. But Gimble told court Wolchock also used the still on the farm of Abraham Toews near Ste. Anne, on Dave Letkeman's farm just southeast of Steinbach, and on J. Kehler's barn one mile west of Steinbach. Court was also shown pictures of warehouses and buildings around Winnipeg, including St. Boniface, used in Wolchock's illegal liquor business. Gimble also alleged Wolchock operated another still on a farm near Stonewall. He said it produced 5,000 gallons of alcohol that summer of 1940.

Wolchock and seven of his partners were convicted but it took three trials. The first trial was declared a mistrial due to suspicion of jury tampering. In the second trial, proceedings were halted when Wolchock required a hernia operation. Finally, he was sent to jail.

He got five years in Stony Mountain Penitentiary, and that was before there was such a thing as parole. It is the most severe sentence ever laid in Manitoba history for a liquor offense. Up to that point in March of

• RCMP raided this substantial farm still east of Winnipeg.

• Mounties' patrol cars were usually no match for rum-runners' souped-up autos.

1940, no one had ever received more than an eight-month sentence for liquor offenses in Manitoba. Also convicted and sentenced were: Ned Balakowski, three years; Ben Balakowski, eight months; Frank McGirl, eight months; Jules Mourant, one year. Sam Arbourg, Eugene Mourant and Cass Mourant each received suspended sentences.

After serving his time, Wolchock remembered the people who helped him in prison. A prison guard at Stony Mountain named Mr. Anderson was always kind to Wolchock. When Wolchock finished his prison term, Leonard was sent out every Christmas over to the Anderson household to deliver food and presents.

Wolchock Sr. also gave generously to the Salvation Army. "He was a great guy to the Salvation Army because the Sally Ann was very good to him in jail," said Leonard. His father also saw to it that Leonard took Jewish dishes to the Jewish prisoners in Stony Mountain on the "high holidays."

Wolchock had money left when he got out of jail but the cost of lawyers for three trials drained a lot of it. Wolchock paid everybody's legal fees. His wife Rose managed their family of four young boys while he was in prison for five years, and Wolchock, when he got out, bought the home then called Bardal Estate, formerly owned by Winnipeg funeral director Neil Bardal. It's a large clapboard house at the end of Hawthorne Avenue in North Kildonan, along the river on what is now named Kildonan Drive. "There was a fireplace in every bedroom," Leonard recalled. Wolchock also had money to buy a little company, Canadian Wreckage and Salvage.

But the money wasn't anything like he was used to, and, after a couple years Wolchock called his old mates together for a meeting. He wanted to make one last batch. Who was in? So the men walled off a portion of the Bardal home's basement—two of Wolchock's close friends were bricklayers—and they constructed a still behind the wall. There were no neighbours on Kildonan Drive at the time so there was no one to detect the smell from alcohol production. The men made the alcohol, distributed it to people they could trust, and dismantled the operation. Then they rode off into the sunset.

"The old man had a bundle of money, and he dished out to everyone. Louis went to Sudbury and got a 7-Up franchise; Charlie went to California and bought a liquor store; Benny G. bought a trucking company; Benny B. moved to Vancouver; Ned went back to work." There were others involved, but Leonard doesn't know what became of them. Other partners had already taken their money and invested before the RCMP arrest: Johnny B. moved to Vancouver and bought a furniture store; Fred S. bought a retail fish store in Winnipeg that still exists today under different owners; another partner went into the hotel business.

And Wolchock? "My dad started Capital Lumber at 92 Higgins Avenue with a partner," said Leonard. "He didn't make money like in the past but he still called the shots and had a successful little business."

That was Prohibition.

"There was honour among men back then. Your word was your bond. Nothing was written down. Everything was a handshake," said Leonard.

"My dad came to this country and he always called it the land of milk and honey. He always said that. He said it after he got out of prison, too. He was never bitter."

Archibald William Wolchock died in 1976 at age 78.

THE DEVIL MADE ME DO IT

January 29, 1932, saw one of the most horrific murders in Manitoba history in the small railway town of Elma, about 100 kilometres east of Winnipeg. The farm family of Martin Sitar, 66, his wife and five children were axed to death in their beds. The murderer then set fire to their home. Sitar's four-year-old son survived for several days before succumbing. While in hospital, he was reported to have mumbled while in a delirious state, "Oh Tom, what are you doing to me?"

RCMP caught farmhand Thomas Hreschkoski who hid out in the snow and bush for five days after the murder. Hreschkoski confessed to the murders, claiming he was commanded to murder the family by "a big black devil with horns, hoof, and tail." He was declared insane and committed to the Selkirk Mental Hospital.

CHAPTER 4

THE STRANGLER

EARLE (THE GORILLA) NELSON

One woman was strangled with her woolen dust rag. Another woman was strangled with laundry pulled off her clothesline. One woman was strangled with the silk cord to her dressing gown. Three women were strangled with kitchen towels. One woman was strangled with her pink tea apron.

The Strangler was leaving a trail of dead across the United States and eventually into Manitoba, turning the trappings of womanhood in the 1920s into murder weapons. The term serial killer was not yet part of our vocabulary.

Every victim was a woman except one time when a mother's infant boy happened to be nearby. In nearly every case, the woman was a landlady with a "Room to Let" sign in her window. The Strangler found his victims by scanning the classified sections. Later, he included women with "House for Sale" signs on their front lawns.

A house with a "Room for Let" sign in the window was a common sight in the 1920s. Many women were made widows in World War One and took in boarders to make ends meet. There weren't welfare or child support payments back then. Married women were the serial killer's victims, too. A working class man's salary

The sight of the sprawled body produced sometimes a scream, sometimes a yell, sometimes a whine.

even back then wasn't enough to support a family, and renting out a room was one way families made some extra cash. Wives usually managed the rental room. The classified ads for the *Manitoba Free Press* back then show as many rooms for rent as apartments.

The serial killer would knock on the door and if a woman answered, he would ask to view the room to let or house for sale.

In every case, the corpse was discovered in a similar manner. Someone couldn't find their wife, their mother, their sister, their daughter, their aunt, their landlady. The person looked for her, called out her name, expected to find her any minute, expected some logical explanation why she couldn't be found. The person went from room to room, then checked the rental rooms. Often the corpse was discovered splayed on the bed or on the floor in a rental. The sight of the sprawled body produced sometimes a scream, sometimes a yell, sometimes a whine. Other times the corpses were found stuffed under a bed or behind the furnace or in a clothes trunk.

Not familiar with serial killers yet as we are today, the newspapers didn't know what to call the murderer: the Dark Strangler, the Beast Man, the Phantom Killer, the Gorilla Man.

A detailed account of his method was provided to police by two women who managed to survive his attacks. Nine women had already been strangled to death when Mrs. H. C. Murray of San Francisco opened her door on November 26, 1926, to a potential buyer for her house. While the West Coast of the United States was under high alert for the Strangler, the hapless man at her door could not be him, Mrs. Murray quickly surmised. "I never once dreamed he was the Strangler," she said later.

This man was pleasant, polite, a little sad. He had a hang-dog expression. He was an avowed Christian and carried about him an elevated sense of decency. She opened the door. She said the man took great interest in details of the room, especially the ceiling. "I realize now that he was try to get me to look up towards the ceiling, so that he could get behind me and grab my throat," she told reporters. At one point, he pulled down a blind in the main bedroom as if to test the roller. The tour ended at the screened porch at the rear of the house. Fortunately, Mrs. Murray, 28, had a rule to keep a distance of six-to-eight feet between herself and potential buyers. "After exhausting every pretense for lingering, he started out," Mrs. Murray said.

But reaching the front door to leave, the man whirled around and asked to view the porch again. Back in the porch, he pointed through the screen to the garage and asked what kind of roof it had. That's when Mrs. Murray made her mistake. She turned her back to him and instantly felt his fingers around her neck. She screamed and tore at his hands with her fingernails. She managed to turn and clawed his face, and then stumbled through the screen door. The man fled and she chased after, hopping onto the running board of a passing vehicle and screaming that she had just been attacked by the Strangler. She was pregnant at the time.

A massive manhunt ensued, with men roaming the streets with shotguns, but the Strangler escaped.

Another woman survived an attack the following spring in Philadelphia. The Strangler had just struck in that city, Apr. 27, 1927, claiming his 16th victim. The next day a man knocked at a door where a home was for sale. A woman in the yard next door called out that the owner wasn't in. The man then asked if her home was the same layout as the one for sale. She said yes. Well, did she mind if he took a look inside? he asked. He was already walking towards the woman. She froze. He lunged at her. She sidestepped and ran inside her house. The Strangler made off again.

He was described as a man of about 30-to-35 years of age, stocky, with dark hair and a sallow complexion. He was a well-dressed working man, said one witness. About five foot, seven inches. He smoked Lucky Strike cigarettes. A San Francisco police chief said: "He is able to gain an amicable footing with women through his suave manner." A Portland grocer, who served the Strangler and only realized it afterward, said he was pleasant, soft-spoken, polite. "Why I never spoke to a nicer mannered fellow," the grocer said.

He had many names, at least 24 by one count, most of which aren't known because the victims didn't live to tell. But among those known are Evan Louis Fuller, Adrian Harris, Mr. Williams, Mr. Woodcocks, Harry Harcourt, Charles Harrison, and Virgil Wilson. He also told people he was Danish by birth, he was separated, his ex-wife had flirted with other men, he was deeply religious. He claimed he was a carpenter, a farm worker, a furnace inspector, a house painter from New York, a bible student, and many other things since he was very adept at making up stories on the spot. He would quote scripture to people.

Much of the information of the Strangler's exploits in the U.S. is gleaned from *Bestial* written by Harold Schechter, a Queens College professor in New York City.

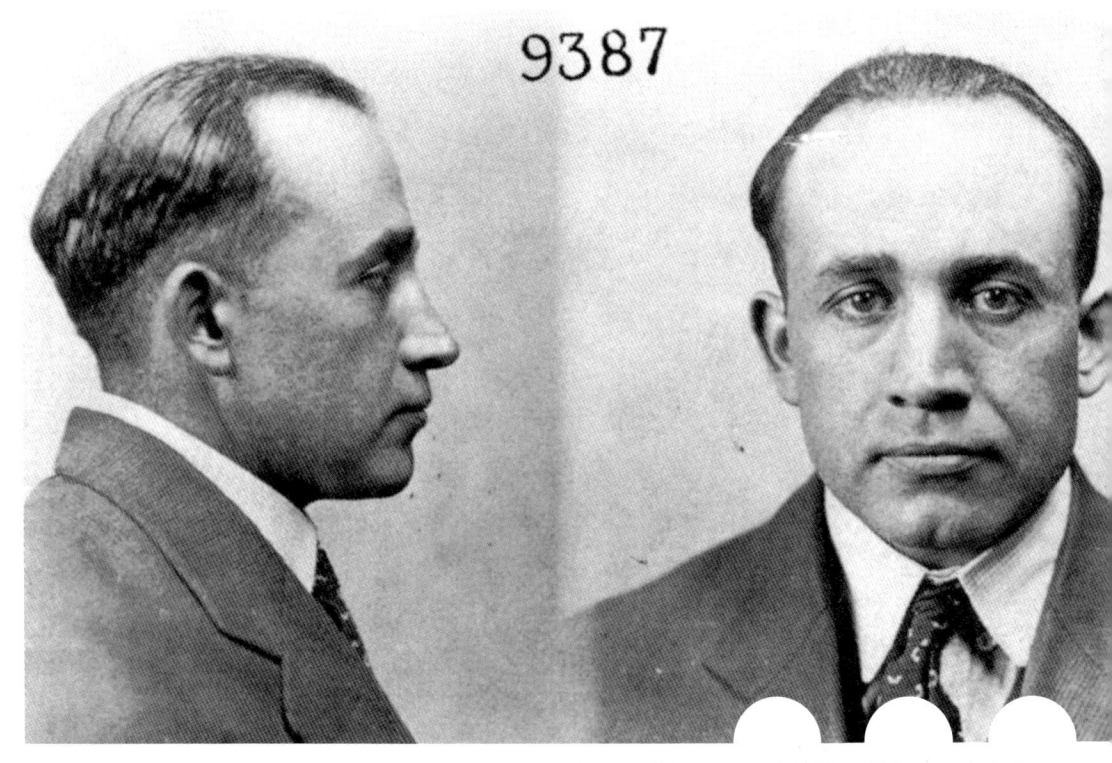

• Like many serial killers, Nelson projected a normal manner and appearance.

CRIMES OF THE CENTURY

The Strangler supported himself at least in part by stealing his victims' jewelry, which would later turn up at sundry pawn shops.

The first of the Strangler's 20 known victims was a 60-year-old woman. The second was 65. The third was 63. In nearly every case, the killer had intercourse with the woman after he'd murdered her. The Strangler supported himself at least in part by stealing his victims' jewelry, which would later turn up at sundry pawn shops.

The trail of murders started in San Francisco, and moved along the West coast, then across the United States. His murders started Feb. 20, 1926. They trail went: San Francisco; San Jose; San Francisco; Santa Barbara; Oakland, Portland; Portland; Portland; San Francisco; Seattle; Portland. Then he started to move across county: Council Bluffs, Iowa; Kansas City, Missouri; Kansas City; Kansas City; Philadelphia; Buffalo; Detroit; Detroit; Chicago.

By the 20th murder, police had no idea where the killer would strike next.

The unassuming stranger walked up the veranda steps at 133 Smith Street in downtown Winnipeg where there was a "Rooms for Let" sign and rapped on the door. It was June 8, 1927. The rooming house was not the way we think of rooming houses today, but was well kept and in good condition. The classified section of a local newspaper, which was found crumpled at a murder scene in Elmwood a few days later, listed it as: "Quiet, LHK Room, BRF, continuous hot water."

The building was owned by Lady Schultz, the widow of former Manitoba Lieutenant Governor Sir John Christian Schultz. The latter Schultz was a physician who campaigned for Manitoba's annexation to Canada—campaigned too hard for Metis leader Louis Riel's liking, who threw him in jail. Schultz escaped six weeks later and moved to Ontario where he became a wealthy businessman, and later returned as a politician and lieutenant governor. Today, the former Schultz property is a parking lot between York Avenue and Broadway.

An elderly couple, Mr. and Mrs. John and Catherine Hill managed the rooming house for the widowed Lady Schultz. In those days, it would probably have been said that Catherine Hill wore the pants in the family. She was a tough, highly proper and highly distrustful woman. You could say she ran a tight ship. She was hyper-vigilant towards boarders, treating them as guilty until they could soften her opinion of them. She treated the dark stranger that way.

"Now mind, I don't allow my roomers to bring any girls or liquor to their rooms," she warned him. The man professed he planned to do nothing of the kind. In fact, he preferred quiet so he could read his bible, he told her. "I am a religious man. I am a Roman Catholic," he replied. Mrs. Hill, 71, was duly impressed.

The man said his name was Mr. Woodcocks and he was working on a construction job across the river in St. Boniface. He and

Mrs. Hill chatted for 20 minutes. Mrs. Hill told her husband later that it wasn't often you heard young men nowadays talk like a Christian. Her husband warned her to be careful. There was some nut running around in the States who talked religious and then killed women, he said.

Who was killing women across North America?

William Morrison, 77, a retired University of Winnipeg sociologist, founded the university's criminology section in the 1960s, and has taught many students about psychological profiling of criminals.

His view on the causes of deviant behaviour can be summed up in a story he tells. "A student of mine, a sweet thing, left from here and continued courses in criminology at Northeastern College in Boston. Her first assignment was to visit the penitentiary there. So she went there, and eight or ten steel doors clang behind her, and they put her in a room with these eight burly, rough-looking prisoners, and just her. 'What did you do?' I asked her. 'I did what you told us to do. I pointed to each one and said, 'Tell me about your father.'"

In Morrison's view, parents are the biggest single influence on whether a person engages in criminal behaviour. That's not a new perspective and it isn't a very sexy one for researchers. But Morrison was a kind of old school sociologist at U of W.

Sociological study of crime has gone through various incarnations. In the 1960s and 70s, it tended towards Marxist theory, citing economic disparity and class struggle as factors shaping criminals. In the 1980s and 90s, there has been great stress on biological factors for crime, ie. genetics. Some social scientists today see almost a genetic pre-determination for crime.

Morrison believes that's dangerous. "Show me the gene (that causes people to kill), and

• Coroner's photo of one of Nelson's Winnipeg victims.

demonstrate to me that everyone who has it, does it. We're more than automatons driven by our genes," he said.

Playing the sleuthing game as if the Strangler were operating right now, Morrison pointed out the obvious. The Strangler carried inside him a rage against his mother. Most of his victims were mother figures, the oldest being 66. In fact, the Strangler married a woman three times his age in 1919, indicative of someone with mother issues. He was just 22 when he wed his 58-year-old bride.

A rage against his mother does not necessarily mean the Strangler's mother was overtly cruel. "She could have been passively sitting there while the father was beating the son to death," Morrison said.

The Strangler carried a sublimated rage. "If they were brought up so that every time they speak out they get hit, they learn to control it and eventually explode," Morrison speculated. He said some disruptive life event had set off the killings. "They suppress or deny their rage until something triggers it," he said. In fact, the murders began after the Strangler's wife left him.

The Strangler's necrophilia is not uncommon among serial killers, although that wouldn't have been known back then, said Morrison. He added the postmortem sex is not about sex but anger. It's to further insult and destroy their victim.

"There are the power rapists and the angry rapists, and this is the angry rapist. They are getting back at women. It's not for sexual satisfaction."

The time lapse between attacks, from months to days, is again typical. "They repress (their urge), but they only repress it for so long. Then it subsides because they've gotten rid of all the rage," he said.

"Most victims are victims of opportunity. The urge reaches the (Strangler) and he strikes out."

Morrison added it is quite common in such cases that the killer wouldn't look like the depraved monster everyone was expecting back in 1926-27. In fact, he would be a bit of a disappointment. Morrison said the serial killer learns how to blend in. They learn how to act, to keep a dual identity. But they are also pathetically insecure. Their actions show their own insecurity and feelings of inadequacy. In fact, the Strangler would become insanely jealous if his much-older wife so much as talked to another man.

"We used to say that when people can't get attention by being good, they get attention by being bad. If they can't get attention by being bad, they look at what is it people value. Property and things. So they either steal property, or destroy it, or burn it up. And if they've got a real rage in them, they take it out on people."

Two modern day psychological profilers, who have written several books on the subject of serial killers, are John Douglas, former chief of the FBI's Investigative Support Unit, and

Robert Ressler, formerly with the FBI's behaviour science unit. Ressler coined the phrase "serial killer" in the mid-80s.

John Douglas, in his book *The Anatomy of Motive*, says serial killers have two factors warring inside: a feeling of superiority, and an equally strong feeling of inadequacy. Douglas maintains there are three early warning signs of a homicidal individual: bed-wetting beyond an appropriate age; fire starting; and cruelty to animals or small children. "The combination of the three were so prominent in our study subjects that we began recommending that a pattern of any two should raise a warning flag for parents and teachers."

The weapon of choice by serial killers is a knife, followed by strangulation, and then suffocation. Ressler believes serial killers tend to not use guns because they want the satisfaction of causing death at hand. Ressler maintains the serial killer repeats the killings because the urge regenerates itself like the sex drive.

Both Douglas and Ressler were part of an FBI study in 1985 that interviewed incarcerated serial killers. The FBI interviewed 36 offenders to find commonalities to help profile future serial killers. The study found 70 per cent of serial killers reported families with histories of alcohol or drug abuse. One-third had histories of psychiatric problems and problems with aggression. Half of serial killers reported criminalized sexual problems within the family. Abuse and neglect was commonplace. About a third of serial killers were witness to sexual violence in their home, and 42 per cent were witness to disturbing sex during formative years. All were subject to emotional abuse during childhood.

Most serial killers masturbate many times a day, and half reported rape fantasies starting at ages 12-14.

Fantasy nearly always precedes the act, according to the study. Violent fantasies occurred in 86 per cent of serial killers. "Once the restraints inhibiting the acting out of the fantasy are no longer present, the individual is likely to engage in a series of progressively more accurate 'trial runs' in an attempt to enact the fantasy as it is imagined. Since the trial runs can never precisely match the fantasy, the need to restage the fantasy with a new victim is established," Douglas and Ressler maintain. However, they stress that most people with violent fantasies don't act them out.

No one knows why serial killers have proliferated in the latter years of the 20th Century. There were virtually none when the Strangler came along. He was making up the role as he went.

The mother's influence on whether a child takes up criminal activity is profound. In 1959, William and Joan McCord and Irving Zola produced a seminal work on how family influences criminal behaviour called Origins of Crime, published by Columbia University Press. The researchers used research by the famous social scientists Sheldon and Eleanor Glueck which followed 253 males from boyhood to adulthood during the Depression and Second World War.

The McCord-Zola findings were often surprising, including that slum neighbourhoods with their inevitable gangs are not causal of crime if a child has a caring parent.

The authors found that love from either parent was important but that the mother's love was a more important socializing force. The problem often was that neglecting mother-types tended to mate with neglecting father-types.

The authors summarized: "We have found that the affection of the parents for their child generally determines the son's chances of becoming a criminal. We have found low crime rates in families reared by either passive or warm fathers, and particularly high criminality in families with neglecting fathers. In families with loving or over-protective mothers we found low crime rates, but in families with passive or neglecting mothers we found a strong tendency towards criminality."

The last finding in particular was stunning. Passive fathers produced low crime rates in sons; passive mothers produced a very high proportion of criminal sons, and the highest proportion of sex offenders of any category of mother. "When the mother is passive, the child's expectations are distinctly violated...The passive, indifferent, withdrawn mother must appear to be rejecting him, when he compares her to his friends' mothers."

"We have found low crime rates in families reared by either passive or warm fathers, and particularly high criminality in families with neglecting fathers..."

By passive, McCord-Zola mean "weak and ineffectual." Passive mothers go through the motions of raising a child but are cold emotionally. They leave discipline up to the father. "An 'I cannot be bothered' attitude governed their relationships with their sons," McCord-Zola said.

"Sexual crime apparently stemmed from thwarted desires for maternal affection."

Hugh and Lola Cowan always went together when selling decorative paper flowers in downtown Winnipeg, except the evening of June 9, 1927. Hugh wasn't feeling well that night, so Lola went alone. Hugh was 12 and Lola was 14. There were six children in the Cowan family.

Lola and her sister Margaret made paper flowers in their bungalow home on University Place, a downtown street across from the old Vaughan Street jail. It is now part of York Avenue. Artificial flower bouquets are made of silk today but back then people used coloured crepe paper. The children would then go knock on doors and sell the flowers for 25 cents a bunch. Downtown Winnipeg was much more residential back then. The children aimed to make a little cash for the family until their father, a salesman, could get back on his feet. He'd been off work several weeks with pneumonia.

That evening, Lola's fair hair was tied up in a bob. She wore a blue pleated skirt and a

MILLION DOLLAR MACHRAY

EMBEZZLEMENT

Any small-time thief can steal $50 from a corner store, but to lift a million requires a pillar of the community. John Machray was just such a man. The nephew of an Anglican Archbishop, and a lawyer, Machray enjoyed an impeccable reputation for integrity. He was a principal in the investment firm of Archibald and Howell, investment managers for the Anglican Archdiocese of Rupertsland, and in 1907 he was appointed to manage all the trust funds of the University of Manitoba, some $500,000 at the time.

• John Machray

It thus developed that as Winnipeg was entering one of its greatest boom times, John Machray had his hand very near to a large cookie jar. Expecting windfall profits from rapidly rising real estate values, Machray, and his partner, Frederick Sharpe, began buying various Winnipeg properties. Spurred by their early successes, Machray began taking on bigger and bigger liabilities. To float this debt, Machray turned to the U of M cookie jar.

Then, in 1912, the three-year real estate boom ended abruptly and the market collapsed. Machray was now sitting on a real estate portfolio in which the liabilities greatly exceeded the value of the properties. Though technically bankrupt, Machray knew that the game would only be up if his clients asked for their money back. So he began moving money around, creating a house of cards that gave the illusion of stability. Aided by feats of bookkeeping legerdemain, and using his reputation and prestige to fend off any enquiries, Machray escaped detection for 20 years.

When the final card toppled in 1932, John Machray was arrested, pleaded guilty to a charge of theft, and was sentenced to seven years. He served little more than a year, dying of cancer in October 1933. When the commission formed to investigate Machray's doings finally sorted through the debris, they found that Machray had misappropriated $869,065.27 from the University, and approximately $1,000,000 from the Anglican Church. This ranks John Machray in the upper echelons of Manitoba's white-collar criminals.

peach-coloured sweater. She'd played baseball after class with chums at Mulvey School earlier that day. She was described as a very quiet and well-mannered girl.

"Oh, she was a lovely person," said her brother Hugh Cowan in an interview. Hugh was 88 at the time of our interview and of failing memory but he was assisted by his wife Lee. He is the last of the Cowan children still alive. "Lola was just a really good person. The whole family was that way," said Hugh. He remembered the night his sister went missing.

"Oh God, that was horrible," recalled Hugh. The Cowans weren't street kids. When she didn't come home, the family went out searching. "I knocked on doors looking for her," Hugh said.

Lee said the disappearance of Hugh's sister plagued her husband all his life. "He wouldn't let me out of his sight. He didn't want it to happen again. And he never let his daughter out of his sight. It caused some problems," said Lee.

Because his sister never would come home. That evening, 14-year-old Lola Cowan happened to stop at a rooming house at 133 Smith Street where a new tenant had checked in: Earle Leonard Nelson.

The Strangler was in town.

The day after murdering and sexually assaulting Lola Cowan, with her corpse still hidden beneath his bed, Earle Nelson decided to sojourn into the suburbs. He crossed the Red River, likely at the Louise Bridge, and strolled around Elmwood. He could have taken a street car across the bridge but likely walked because he had very little money, according to his landlady Mrs. Hill.

He wound up near where the Disraeli Bridge connects to Henderson Highway today. The Disraeli was not yet built, and wouldn't be built until Oct. 20, 1959, when two of Manitoba's most venerable politicians, Mayor Steven Juba and Premier Duff Roblin, officially opened it.

One Elmwood woman later told police a man came to her home at Brazier Street and Riverton Avenue that afternoon of June 10, 1927, claiming to sell soap powder. He was a very pushy salesman, she said. He barged into her house and got as far as her kitchen before the woman threatened to call her husband, who was sleeping in the next room. The man finally left. Later, a resident at 104 Riverton said he saw a stocky, olive-skinned man knock at the house at 100 Riverton, where William and Emily Patterson and their two sons lived.

The Pattersons lived in a little blue house on a row of clapboard houses on Riverton, the first block west at the foot of where the Disraeli Bridge is today. The family had emigrated from Ireland the year before. William worked downtown at the Eaton's store.

Like any immigrants to a country, husband and wife depended heavily on each other. When William returned from work that evening

He was a very pushy salesman, she said. He barged into her house and got as far as her kitchen before the woman threatened to call her husband, who was sleeping in the next room.

and found his wife wasn't home, he knew immediately something was terribly wrong. The boys, ages three and five, hadn't seen their mother since that afternoon.

He asked around the neighbourhood but no one knew where Emily was. He searched, and fretted, and around midnight, fearing the worst, William knelt to pray at the foot of his three-year-old son's bed, asking God to please lead him to his wife. It was then he noticed something under the bed. A leg. A corpse. His beloved wife. Emily Patterson had been strangled and sexually violated like more than 20 women before her.

The mysterious death wasn't connected yet to the Strangler, at least not in the newspapers, but Winnipeg Chief of Police George Smith had a pretty good idea. Smith began reading over circulars he had on file about the Strangler from several American police chiefs. It didn't take long before Smith was convinced the Strangler was in Winnipeg. That happened with the discovery of the second corpse, Lola Cowan.

The public announcement was made Sunday. Local radio programs were interrupted at around 6:30 p.m. to break the news. The broadcast announced that another body had been discovered, and police believed it was the work of the Strangler from the United States. Every man, woman and child was warned not to let any strangers into their home.

The broadcast came after Bernard Mortensen, a downstairs lodger at the Hill rooming house on Smith Street, came to Mrs. Hill very excitedly early that morning, crying in broken English, because he was a Dane and did not speak English well. "Mrs. Hill! Mrs. Hill! Front room! Upstairs!"

Mortensen led Mrs. Hill, who walked with a cane, upstairs to the room vacated by a Mr. Woodcocks. The door was ajar. There the Danish lodger pointed to the naked body of Lola Cowan stuffed under the bed.

RIDING MOUNTAIN REVENGE

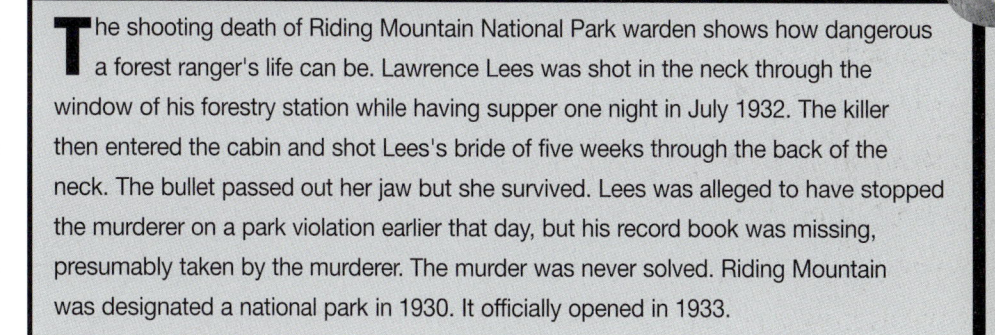

The shooting death of Riding Mountain National Park warden shows how dangerous a forest ranger's life can be. Lawrence Lees was shot in the neck through the window of his forestry station while having supper one night in July 1932. The killer then entered the cabin and shot Lees's bride of five weeks through the back of the neck. The bullet passed out her jaw but she survived. Lees was alleged to have stopped the murderer on a park violation earlier that day, but his record book was missing, presumably taken by the murderer. The murder was never solved. Riding Mountain was designated a national park in 1930. It officially opened in 1933.

"Someone dead in my house!" cried out Mrs. Hill.

"My poor girl," sobbed Mrs. Cowan to a reporter.

If you drive into the Elmwood Cemetery off of Hespeler Avenue, there is a headstone on your right hand side a short ways inside the gates. The brown headstone is for Lola Margaret Beaulah Cowan. "Safe in the arms of Jesus," reads the inscription. It adds that the headstone was erected by pupils of Mulvey

Schools. Lola's classmates helped raised money to mark their friend Lola's grave.

Emily Patterson is also buried in Elmwood Cemetery but her grave is unmarked. That seems a terrible shame. Her husband likely couldn't afford a headstone. It is believed he returned to Ireland right after the trial because there is no record of him in Winnipeg,. At the trial into his wife's murder, William Patterson would break down during testimony, his voice falling to a whisper until nothing came out at all. The judge allowed him to step down when it became obvious he could no longer continue.

Elmwood Cemetery records show where Emily Patterson is buried. Her gravesite is about a block away from where she and her family hoped to start a new life in Winnipeg. She and Lola Cowan are buried side by side.

Winnipeg Police Chief George Smith must have brooded over the great manswarm that rushed outside his window in downtown Winnipeg. Somewhere out there was the Strangler. Somewhere out there, in his proverbial back yard, was the villain of the century to that point. He had one thought, get him, and it shut every other thought down. All those things that weren't important, weren't important. All those things that shouldn't matter but did, didn't. He looked out the window over the sweetness of Manitoba in June, and the sweetness of Manitoban women. Then he relived seeing the corpses of the two innocent young women. Smith would not sleep again for the better part of a week. Get him.

Every officer was available. Smith's plan was simply to leave no stone unturned. He ordered his officers to chase down every lead, no matter how implausible, and there were hundreds of alleged tips. But it wasn't just the police. Every Manitoban had the same thought. There was no should we or shouldn't we. Husbands who ignored their wives suddenly were willing to lay down their lives for them. Wives who had grown weary of their husbands now saw something brave and noble in them. At night, Winnipeg streets were eerily empty as people heeded police warnings to stay inside.

Make no mistake, the Strangler was the Ripper of his time. He didn't eviscerate his victims like Jack the Ripper but his attacks struck deeper into the continent's psyche. His victims were middle-class moms and housewives, not the trulls of seedy Whitechapel District that Jack the Ripper roamed. The Strangler attacked women right in their homes.

Earle Nelson lit out of town Friday, before Smith launched his manhunt, and headed west. He hitchhiked and walked. Nelson had a car in the U.S. but had ditched it before he crossed the border. After leaving Winnipeg, he stopped in Headingley and bought a new fedora. He stopped in Austin and discarded the suit of clothes he was wearing for a pair of blue overalls with bib and a khaki shirt. He got as far as Regina where he rented a room under the name Harry Harcourt and took the landlady's daughter out for a soda. The daughter became scared of him and made up an excuse to get away from him. Winnipeg police were contacted by several drivers who had given a lift to a stranger who fit the description of Nelson. They said he was headed west, and police chief Smith notified colleagues in Saskatchewan and Alberta. In Alberta, police sealed off every road leading into the province. But Nelson had already started to double back into Manitoba. He crossed back inside the Manitoba border, then headed south, presumably trying to return to the United States. He bought a straw hat in Boissevain. He stopped at a restaurant in the small town of Wapoka, just six kilometers from the border.

Several people in Manitoba thought he fit the description of the Strangler and contacted the Winnipeg and Manitoba Provincial Police, including a Main Street pawn shop owner who said the description fit a man who sold him some jewelry. The jewelry turned out to belong to Emily Patterson.

People in southwestern Manitoba were already giving chase, hoping to net the $1,500 reward for Nelson's capture. Two farmers hot on his trail got their truck stuck on a muddy road and had to abandon their pursuit.

Nelson stopped at a general store in Wakopa run by Leslie Morgan and bought a hunk of cheddar cheese, two bottles of cola, and a pack of Millbank cigarettes. Morgan served Nelson but phoned the police after Nelson left. Then Morgan and some other residents formed two posses and gave chase. However, Nelson veered off the main road and gave them the slip.

Manitoba Provincial Police Constable Wilton Grey and his partner named Sewell arrested Nelson heading south about two kilometers from the Morgan store. Nelson claimed his name was Virgil Wilson from Vancouver, and that he'd been working on a ranch owned by someone named George Harrison near Wakopa the past three months. The other residents from Wakopa caught up with the officers and said there was no rancher named George Harrison in the area.

On the drive to a Killarney jail, Nelson claimed he was born in Lancashire, England, to an English mother and Spanish father. It was after 8 p.m. by the time they had Nelson in the Killarney jail. His cell had two padlocks. The constables could have been heroes except for one oversight. They left a nail file where Nelson could reach it by stretching his arm between the bars. Nelson was an adept lock picker who had broken out of an asylum for the insane in San Francisco several times. He sprang the locks in a matter of minutes and was on the loose again.

Police Chief Smith's elation over Nelson's suspected capture didn't last long. He got word of Nelson's escape from a *Manitoba Free Press* reporter, who telephoned him directly with the

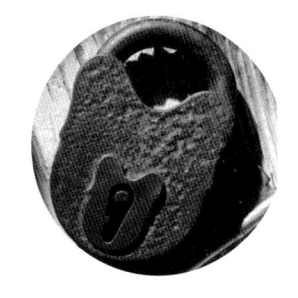

They left a nail file where Nelson could reach it by stretching his arm between the bars. Nelson was an adept lock picker who had broken out of an asylum for the insane in San Francisco several times.

CRIMES OF THE CENTURY

There are two kinds of serial killer, the charming, talkative types filled with seething resentment that the world doesn't recognize their greatness; and the quiet loner sinking into oblivion who makes a despicable stab at notoriety.

news around midnight. The *Free Press* had staffed the news room 24 hours a day since the Strangler murders. Smith quickly rounded up 20 men and a team of bloodhounds and caught a special 2:45 a.m. train to Killarney. A *Free Press* correspondent was on board. When the team of police officers arrived at Killarney later that morning, who should be there but Nelson hoping to catch the train. Nelson had slept under the railway platform and crawled out when he heard the train coming, hoping to slip aboard unnoticed. Fat chance. The officers quickly surrounded him. Nelson bolted through them like a wild animal. He was tackled from behind by Constable William Renton of the Crystal City detachment of the Manitoba Provincial Police.

He was not what anyone expected. Nelson was disarmingly relaxed and at peace with himself on the train ride back to Winnipeg. He joked and told "foul stories," the *Free Press* correspondent reported. Nelson didn't seem like a serial murderer, according to the reporter. "'Are you sure you have the right man?' was on a hundred lips," the correspondent wrote.

But Smith knew. He repeatedly assured officers and the public that police had their man. Crowds gathered at the railway stop in Winnipeg hoping to catch a glimpse of the monster. In one *Free Press* photo, several women stand in front while Nelson is marched past in handcuffs. The women wear those flapper-style hats that look like bathing caps with brims. Their eyes glower with disgust. The *Free Press* described it as "vengeful" looks they cast at the suspect. The *Free Press* used new motion picture technology to record the police car containing Nelson as it drove into the police garage. It was one of those applications of technology destined not to survive. It just looks like 25 frames of the same police car over and over again.

With Nelson finally behind bars, the Winnipeg police telegrammed an International Anti-Crime Conference in Nelson, British Columbia with the news. The auditorium erupted with applause. Acting police chief Philip Stark made a statement, thanking the many people responsible for helping with the capture, including provincial police forces in all three Prairie provinces. He also thanked the railways, Canadian Pacific and Canadian National, for making their resources available. He thanked the T. Eaton Company, which loaned police a dozen cars for the search. But Stark saved his biggest thanks for Police Chief Smith, who by then was presumably already at home and fast asleep in bed. Stark said the police chief hadn't slept since Emily Patterson's body was found strangled almost a week earlier. Smith wasn't the only one who slept well that night. The entire province did.

Harold Schechter, who wrote *Bestial, The Story of Earle Nelson*, explains how Nelson was dubbed the "Gorilla Man" by some people. North America had apes on the brain in the mid-1920s, Schechter said. Darwin's *Origin of the Species* was published in 1859, but it was still trying to break into mainstream society. The controversial "Monkey Trial" of a Tennessee school teacher John Scopes for teaching Darwin's theory of evolution took place in 1925. About the same time, famous Tarzan writer Edgar Rice Burroughs wrote *The Hairy Ape*, and Lon Chaney was mutating into a simian beast in *A Blind Bargain*. A Broadway hit called *The Gorilla* also opened in 1925.

Manitobans discovered that Nelson, viewed up close, was a disappointment, the way most serial killers are. In fact, from what we know now, serial killers are almost stereotypical. There are two kinds of serial killer, the charming, talkative types filled with seething resentment that the world doesn't recognize their greatness; and the quiet loner sinking into oblivion who makes a despicable stab at notoriety. Nelson was the latter. He was a mess, in and out of asylums in the U.S. Before he starting killing women, he had gone to jail for the sexual assault of a young girl, the way a lot of serial killers start out. Like all serial killers, he was unable to obtain mature, consensual relationships with other adults. But he liked to follow his macabre exploits in the newspapers.

Dr. Morrison's prognosis was correct. Nelson had a mother complex. Nelson's birth mother died of syphilis when he was just nine and a half months old. His father died of the same disease seven months later. He was obviously not born into a happy household.

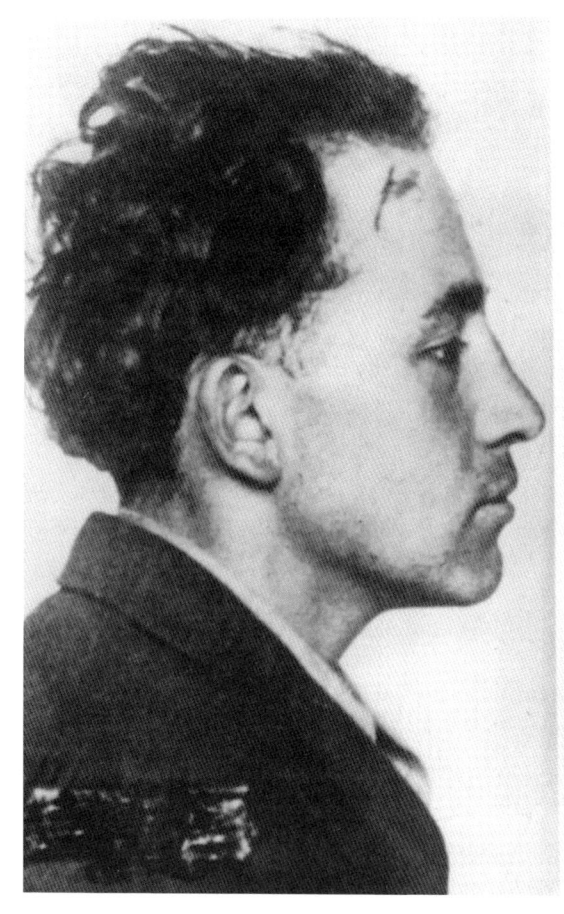

It isn't known if Nelson had congenital syphilis from his parents, which can cause birth defects, but he was diagnosed with syphilis when he was in his 20s. He definitely had mental problems, yet syphilis more regularly leads to physical deformities and vision problems, rather than brain deformities. A glazed look would often come over Nelson, and he seemed mildly retarded, which sounds possibly like fetal alcohol syndrome or fetal alcohol effects.

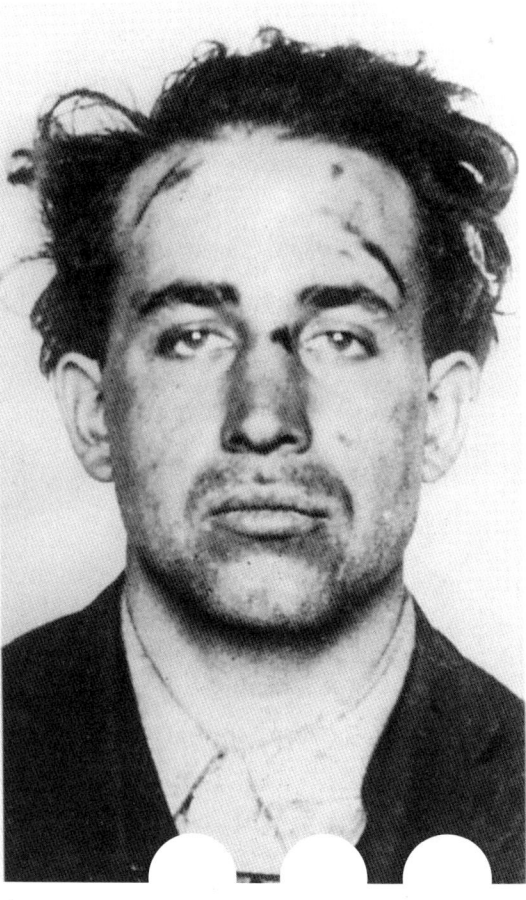

• Nelson looked a little worse for wear after his arrest by American police.

By some twisted logic, he thought by killing mother figures he was ridding the world of evil when in fact he was the evil.

It may not seem like a scenario for a child to build up a hate towards the mother, when the mother dies before a child is a year old. In fact, that is exactly when a child feels the mother's loss the greatest, according to psychological childhood trauma experts. The child feels the loss of the mother, and feels anger towards her for leaving. It doesn't matter the actual reason, it's only the leaving that matters.

That feeling is deepened if Nelson felt his mother's leaving was her own ill-doing. For example, if his next guardian happens to be very religious and privately blames the mother for what has happened to the child, that feeling would carry through to the child. That's what occurred. Nelson was taken over by his grandmother. There is some dispute over whether she was his paternal or maternal grandmother but it doesn't likely matter. What is significant is she was a fire and brimstone religious type. It's from her that Nelson got his fascination with biblical scripture. He glommed onto that idea that his mother's leaving was brought on by herself, and that she was evil. By some twisted logic, he thought by killing mother figures he was ridding the world of evil when in fact he was the evil.

"I've been unfortunate from the day of my birth," Nelson said the day before his execution to a *Manitoba Free Press* reporter. "I've been handicapped by the sins of my parents, who left a taint in my blood that's caused me all kinds of agony of body and mind."

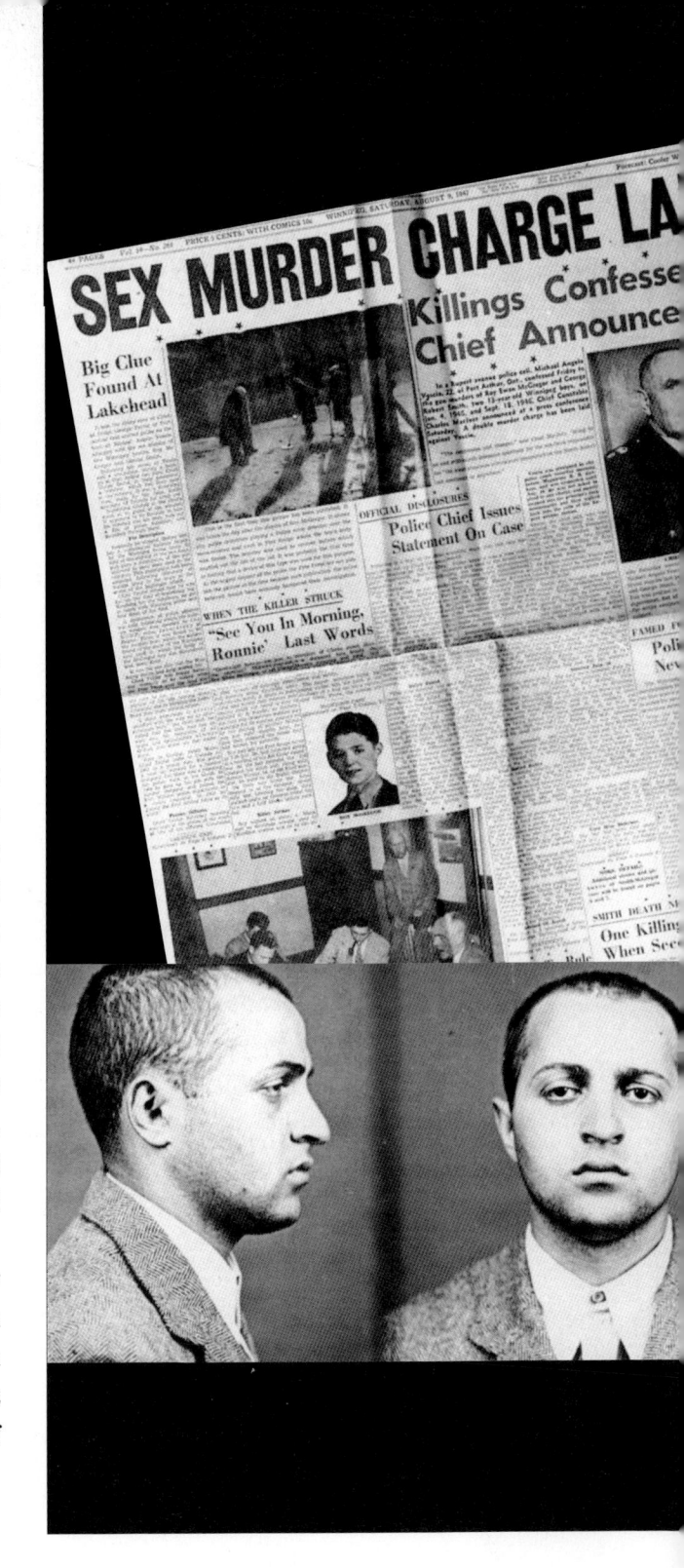

THE NIGHT STALKER

SEX MURDER

On the morning of January 5, 1946, workers at Moore's coal yard in Winnipeg made a grim discovery. In a bin they found the frozen body of Roy Ewan McGregor. Only 13 years of age, McGregor had been bound, sexually assaulted, and shot, once in the stomach, and once in the forehead. The senseless brutality of the killing stunned the city, and police were under tremendous pressure to bring the culprit to justice quickly. It was not to be easy.

Although he had been left in the bin, the murder had taken place some 70 yards away, and both bullets had gone right through his body. Finding them would be next to impossible in the heavy blanket of snow. Faced with this, Detective Inspector Bill McPherson called upon his wartime experience with the Royal Canadian Engineers. He suggested combing the area with a mine detector. This is believed to be the first time a mine detector was used in this manner.

After three days of painstaking searching in -20°C weather, police finally located a single bullet. A ballistics test showed the bullet to be from a 9mm Browning pistol made by the John Inglis Company of Toronto. This initial success was short-lived, however, and police ran into a wall in their attempts to identify a suspect.

Then, the unthinkable happened. Another young boy was found murdered in the lane behind 626 Home Street. George Smith's ankles had been tied up, just as McGregor's were, he had been sodomized, and shot in the heart with what would later prove to be the same weapon. Public outrage hit fever pitch, and police departments all over North America were enlisted to help find the depraved killer. Once again, police were unable to come up with even a suspect, and the investigation languished for a further nine months.

In the midst of despair at not being able to solve two vicious homicides, the good guys finally got the break they needed, and it was old-fashioned police diligence that gave it to them. On June 30, 1947, Port Arthur police arrested two men for robbing a local dairy. Both men had been armed, and the Chief of Police, George Taylor, recalled the Winnipeg Police bulletin regarding the Winnipeg murders. He also remembered that one of the men, Michael Vescio, had seemed very anxious about being caught with his gun. Taylor dug out the bulletin, and found that Vescio's weapon was exactly the type used in the Winnipeg homicides. He immediately called Chief MacIver.

On July 19, the RCMP crime lab in Regina confirmed that Vescio's gun was the same as that used to kill McGregor and Smith. After 18 frustrating months, police finally had their man. Confronted with this evidence, Vescio soon confessed to both killings. A week after the start of his trial, the jury came back with a guilty verdict. The sentence was death, and on November 19, 1948, with a flick of his wrist, Arthur Ellis dispatched Michael Vescio to the void below.

• Police use mine detector to search for clues.

He told the reporter he would devote the rest of his life to the study of religion if his sentence was commuted, although he realized that was unlikely to happen.

Nelson stood trial in Winnipeg for the murder of Emily Patterson. He looked bored throughout. He sat and yawned and sometimes slept through proceedings. Nelson's wife testified that Nelson believed he looked like Jesus Christ, and perhaps that explained his disinterest in the trial. There was a tremendous amount of evidence against him. Virtually everyone he had contact with, including women in the U.S., picked him out of a police lineup.

The only question was whether Nelson was criminally insane. Prosecution pointed to his repeated change of clothes after a murder so as to elude authorities, as evidence that he realized what he had done was wrong. The legal definition of insanity is an inability to appreciate the logical and probable consequences of one's actions.

Nelson declared his innocence to the end, including in the interview granted with the *Free Press* the day before his execution. He claimed he was never even in Winnipeg until police arrested him and brought him to the city. He told the reporter he would devote the rest of his life to the study of religion if his sentence was commuted, although he realized that was unlikely to happen.

In an interview with the *Winnipeg Tribune*, Nelson tried to explain his wanderlust across the United States and into Manitoba. "I admit that I am subject to spells of lunacy in which I function the same as in a dream and sometimes find myself in strange places. But I never hurt anyone in these spells," he proclaimed.

Allan C. Carlisle, a retired American psychologist who worked with prison inmates including famous serial killers Ted Bundy and Arthur Bishop, maintains serial killers develop Dr. Jekyll-Mr. Hyde personalities: a face for the outer world, and a harboured dark side in private that resorts to violent fantasy to escape childhood trauma.

These are not split personalities, but divided personalities, he says in his book *The Divided Self: Toward an Understanding of the Dark Side of the Serial Killer*. Carlisle believes some stress causes the violent murder and sex fantasies to gain ground and start to take over the person's good side.

"Ongoing and intense fantasy is a mechanism by which hate and bitterness can begin to become disassociated and compartmentalized from the more ethically focused aspects of the mind," he maintains. The danger is when an opportunity arises to act out the violent fantasy and the person crosses the line into their fantasy life. "By acting out the fantasy, the dark side or Shadow, now becomes a more permanent part of the person's personality structure."

The violent act itself is like the fantasy. "When a person is absorbed in a fantasy, he disassociates everything around him. Anger and emptiness become the energy and motivating forces behind the fantasy," Carlisle writes.

"The only way he can handle the guilt is to compartmentalize it and thus not consciously experience it."

Nelson reached a state where he could completely compartmentalize his evil acts, and live in total denial of them. However, it would seem wrong to think that he lapsed into some hypnotic state during the murders and wasn't aware of his actions. After all, what was he doing at various pawn shops the day after the murders selling off the victim's jewelry? Where did he think the jewelry came from?

One final theory is tossed out by Schechter, the Queens College professor who has written biographies on serial killers. Schechter wonders if part of Nelson's problems stemmed from a head injury suffered as a child. To impress friends, a young Nelson crossed the trolley tracks in front of a trolley but the trolley caught his rear tire and sent him sprawling. He landed headfirst on cobblestones, and was unconscious for almost a week.

Recent studies suggest head injuries can lead to deviant behaviour. A study by the Institute for Child Health in London, England reported in 2000 that damage to the ventral region of the frontal lobe of the brain—just above the eye sockets—seems to have caused some people long-term behavioural problems. Of the two subjects studied, one was expelled from school as a threat to other students, and the other developed drink and drug problems.

The ventral part of the frontal lobes is believed to control impulsive desires, the Institute of Child Health said. Loss of it leads to deviant behaviour. "We may be able to identify such cases in future, by brain scans following the accident," said lead researcher Professor Faraneh Vargha-Khadem. "Not only might we be warned of such future problems but we may be able to correct them."

In other words, researchers may one day argue that Earle Nelson was turned into a killer by a bump on the head.

It was fast justice back then. Nelson was arrested in June, convicted in November, and hanged on January 13, 1928. His last words were: "I am innocent. I stand innocent before God and man. I forgive those who have wronged me and ask forgiveness of those I have injured. God have mercy!" ⊙

CHAPTER 5

THE GREAT GOLD ROBBERY

FLYING BANDIT KEN LEISHMAN

Ken Leishman, the Flying Bandit, looked around for a place to stash his 11 gold bars. Why not? he must have thought, smiling beneath his pencil-thin moustache. So he dropped the gold bricks into a snowbank in a Winnipeg backyard at 119 Balfour Street in Riverview. Each bar weighed about 70 pounds and sank heavily to the frozen ground. Leishman tossed some snow overtop the gold and left.

Then it began to snow. March 4, 1966, marked the snowstorm of the century in Winnipeg. It snowed like there was no tomorrow. It snowed like some biblical decree. The mound of snow covering the stash of gold grew to one foot, two feet, three feet, four.

About 15 inches fell in about 24 hours but more important was the way it fell. A 110 kilometre per hour wind whipped the snow into towering moraines. Snowdrifts 15 feet high were common. CKY Television staff measured one snowdrift 19 feet high, station broadcaster Ray Torgrud told the *Winnipeg Free Press*. Meteorologists compared the winds to a hurricane blowing off the ocean.

The Winnipeg Police Chief, whose name coincidentally was George Blow, warned everyone to stay inside until the blizzard was over. Mayor Steve Juba echoed that. "They're taking their lives into their own hands," Juba said.

There were 135 city transit buses stranded in that snowstorm. Six buses alone were stuck on Portage Avenue between Fort and Carlton Streets. On one city bus, passengers sat 13 hours while the driver kept the engine going and the heat

CRIMES OF THE CENTURY

...in newspapers, and Letters to the Editor, and on phone-in radio shows, Winnipeggers tipped their hats to the genius and bravado of the criminals.

blasting. Other passengers simply knocked on the door of the nearest home and were taken in.

All schools closed, as did all stores, as were all highways, as were all airport runways, as were all businesses except emergency services. Firemen on their way to fires got stuck. People who tried to dig out their cars saw the snow backfill as fast as they could shovel it out. The *Winnipeg Free Press* said southern Manitoba had "buckled at the knees."

And the snow whipped and rolled and scudded over the 11 gold bars.

At the downtown Eatons and Bay department stores, over 1,600 stranded staff and shoppers spent the night together. At Eatons, men slept on the ninth floor, women on the seventh. They had lots of television sets and beds and games to keep up spirits, an Eatons manager said.

Winnipeggers typically grumbled about the weather, then turned it into a big excuse to party. Downtown bars and restaurants catered to thousands of stranded people, and ran out of food and in some cases liquor. The Viscount Gort Hotel reported more than 100 stranded customers held a sing-song in the bar. At the Airport Hotel on Ellice Avenue, 20 people slept on the beverage room floor. Ten people bedded down in a Polo Park barber shop. "Laughter was loud. It was more like an office Christmas party," was how one scene was described by a *Winnipeg Free Press* reporter.

The sky cleared Saturday and Winnipegers were freed. Kids burrowed tunnels and forts, and slid down giant hard-packed snowdrifts. Some lucky children could scale snowdrifts and climb onto their roofs. Then they would cannonball off and drifted snow would break their fall.

One of those drifts hid the fortune in gold bricks stashed by Ken Leishman, probably the most renowned criminal in Manitoba history. Leishman masterminded the Great Gold Robbery—a robbery on scale with the Brinks Robbery in Boston in 1950, and the Great Train Robbery in Britain in 1963. No one knew yet that Leishman was behind the theft. But in newspapers, and Letters to the Editor, and on phone-in radio shows, Winnipeggers tipped their hats to the genius and bravado of the criminals.

Media at the time calculated the gold bars stolen from Winnipeg International Airport were worth $382,436.28. However, that grossly underestimated the real gold market. Dan Anderson, who was a University of Manitoba geology professor at the time and who spent many years in gold mining, still laughs at that figure. "You could take that $382,000 and multiply it by 10. The gold was worth more like $3-$4 million," said Anderson.

The reason is gold sales and gold prices were still controlled by Western governments in 1966. Western governments set an artificially low gold price for their own trade, and used gold as a hedge against inflation and financial collapse. At the government-set prices of $37.70 per Troy ounce, Leishman's cargo was worth

$382,000. But the government was the last place Leishman planned to sell it to, even if he could sell it there. The black market was the real market. Even in the United States, the black market paid many times the government price, and in places like India, Pakistan and Asian countries, where Leishman had a plane ticket to, buyers paid 10 times the Western government price.

When Western governments finally let gold float on the open market in 1975, the price instantly shot to $125 per ounce, a truer reflection of its market value; gold surpassed $800 an ounce by 1980; it hovered at about $300 per ounce at the time of this writing.

To put the gold robbery into today's terms, simply note that inflation has increased the value of a 1966 dollar almost six times. One dollar in 1966 has the purchasing power of almost $6 today. In other words, Leishman's $4 million gold robbery would be worth over $20 million in today's dollars. Now that's a heist.

It's also a lot of money to leave in a snowbank. The gold bricks must have glowed like a hearth beneath the snow. When the storm finally stopped, the gold lay beneath an eight-foot high snowdrift.

Ken Leishman once belonged to the North Winnipeg Rotary Club that was responsible for building the original Rainbow Stage in Winnipeg's Kildonan Park. He was a good speaker, too. That was after he'd been convicted and gone to jail as the Flying Bandit but before the Great Gold Robbery at Winnipeg International Airport. His rotary club membership just goes to show how ensconced in the local community he was. Everyone knew him. He was always on the go. He was one of those indefatigable people. Most people couldn't keep up with him.

He was also very bright. Everyone noticed. He is reported to have had an IQ of 146. The average IQ score is 105 for an adult.

And he was a friendly man. He's probably the only criminal who is almost a role model except for his being a thief. He was good at heart and a man of his word.

"He was a heck of a good neighbour," said Cyril Deane. The Deane family lived across the street from the Leishman family on Mark Pearce Avenue in North Kildonan. City councillor Mark Lubosh now lives in the Leishman house.

"Ken was a big man (6'2", 215 pounds), and he was very friendly, and he was always a gentleman," said Pauline Deane, Cyril's wife. "If Cyril was out raking the lawn, Ken would come over and help him. That's the kind of guy he was. He'd do anything for you."

Leishman liked to talk, Pauline said.

"He was exuberant but he wasn't loud. He was gung ho about everything. His problem was he wanted everything tomorrow," she said.

Everyone knew about his history as the Flying Bandit, yet none of the neighbours asked

MOGGEY'S MEANDERINGS

ARMED ROBBERY

Percy Moggey was born in the Portage la Prairie district in the year 1904. As a young man, he surveyed his limited career prospects and decided on crime. His record in his chosen field was lengthy, spanning close to 50 years, and in 1961, he was named to Canada's Most Wanted Criminals list.

Young Moggey apprenticed as a housebreaker, moved into armed robbery, and in 1924, after wounding two Winnipeg police officers, was sentenced to 10 years in Stony Mountain Penitentiary. But Percy Moggey was not a man who liked to take time off work, so naturally he tried to escape. He failed, and had another 18 months tacked on to his sentence. He was released in 1934, and in 1935 shot another two policemen who had the effrontery to try and arrest him for robbery. The judge said 13 years, and then two more for a 1937 escape attempt.

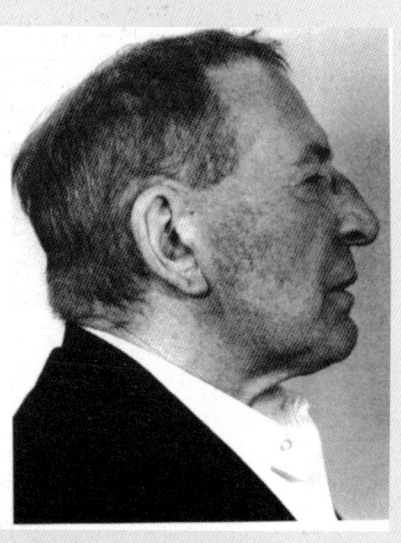

They let him out in 1947, and Percy went right back to work. In 1948, he returned to Stony Mountain for possessing housebreaking tools and explosives. True to form, Percy tried to escape. This time he actually made it, but only for two hours. When he was released in 1953, Percy stayed out of jail for four long years, a personal best. Alas, in 1957 Percy drew 10 for breaking and entering, no surprise there.

By this time, Percy was pretty familiar with Stony, so one night he tucked a dummy into his bed, forced three cell block doors, climbed over the 18-foot wall—a first—and vanished. The ensuing manhunt lasted 10 months. Percy was "seen" in Florida, and British Columbia. In reality, he was hiding out in a cabin he built in the bush near Eriksdale, Manitoba. Always discreet, Percy refused to say where he got the furnishings for his cabin, which included a radio, so he could follow the police search. Percy may have been a fugitive, but a fellow has to get out now and then, and he visited taverns in nearby Moosehorn, and also in Teulon and Arborg. Moggey got his hands on a .22 rifle to put meat on the table, and he also trapped muskrat. Life was not luxurious, but at least the sunlight wasn't striped.

Lady Luck turned her back on Percy in June. Some local Indians searching for seneca root came upon Percy and his shack. They chatted, and when Percy allowed as how he didn't know what seneca root was, his visitors knew he wasn't a local. They called the RCMP, and on June 10, they popped in on Percy, unannounced. Given Moggey's penchant for shooting cops who tried to arrest him, they were expecting the worst. This time however, Percy was most gracious. He offered no resistance, and even offered his guests some tea.

So once again, Percy took up residence at Stony Mountain, but his wandering days were over. He served out his time, and was released in 1967. But wouldn't you know it, one year later Percy got nabbed for…breaking and entering. No doubt the warden had kept the light on in Percy's cell, and back he went. Meanwhile his humble country abode had become a mecca for tourists. They cleared a road through the bush, named it Moggey's Road, took pictures, and there was some discussion about preserving the site.

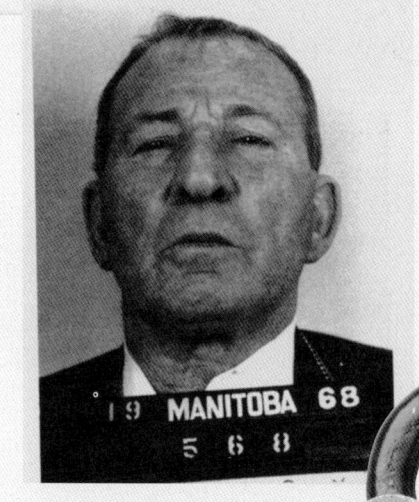

This last brush with the law proved to be Percy's swan song. He had a stroke in 1970, and in 1974 suffered a fatal cerebral haemorrhage. At age 69, Percy Moggey finally retired from his lifelong profession.

Winnipeg Free Press

WINNIPEG, MONDAY, JULY 25, 1960

HELICOPTER IN SEARCH

'Houdini' Prison Break Baffles Mounties, Dog

A prisoner described as a "lone wolf" and possibly dangerous broke out of Stony Mountain Penitentiary early Monday, his second escape from Stony Mountain.

Road blocks have been staked surrounding the Stony Mountain-Winnipeg areas. Between RCMP officers are conducting search.

in the province have RCMP are questioning of the Stony

TERM

prisoner, Percy Moggey rving a 10-year term charges of breaking, ing and theft; trespassing and carrying a weapon. He forced his way out of his cell sometime during the night.

Warden C. E. Desroches said a prison officer discovered him missing from his cell about 3 a.m. and RCMP were called to conduct the search.

It is believed Moggey was not armed when he escaped. He went out through the prison kitchen and scaled the northeast wall with a hook and

Authorities said Moggey "might be considered dangerous." The 56-year-old prisoner has a record dating back to 1924.

FLED IN '49

He received his current sentence in November, 1957, at Port Arthur, Ont. Born in Portage la Prairie, Man., he had spent most of his life in the Port Arthur area.

While serving a term in Stony Mountain in 1949, Moggey escaped for "a short time."

The following description of the prisoner was issued by the penitentiary: 56 years old, 160 to 165 pounds, 5 ft. 6½ inches tall, fresh, ruddy complexion, brown hair, grey eyes and a scar on the left side of his nose.

He was wearing prison clothing — khaki trousers, blue striped shirt and black shoes.

There was no suggestion of outside assistance, an RCMP official said.

One official said he doubted Moggey would head for Winnipeg. He was not the type to go into the city.

Since his first prison term the longest Moggey has spent outside prison walls was four years from 1953 to 1957.

He was sentenced for one violent crime — wounding with intent — 25 years ago.

72

...he bought a cheap old canvas airplane and took flying lessons. Soon he was landing in farmers' fields with a plane full of farm parts.

about it. Despite his past, people knew they could trust Leishman.

"You could leave $200 on the table and go away for a week, and he wouldn't touch it," Pauline said.

Leishman did have a penchant for stealing from big companies.

"He didn't steal from individuals. In that way he was honest," said Blair Leishman, the fifth of Leishman's seven children. "He didn't steal from homes or from peoples' wallets. But he thought it was OK to steal from a big bank because that stuff is insured."

The oldest Leishman kids would baby-sit the Deanes' kids. They wouldn't just baby-sit but clean the house, do the dishes, pick up the toys. Cyril and Pauline never ceased to be astonished when they arrived home. "They had the nicest kids on the street. They were the most well-behaved kids," said Pauline.

Pauline added that the stories about Ken and Elva are true: they acted like young lovers all the time. "They were always sitting together with their arms around each other, even six kids later. Ken was devoted to Elva. I guess that's why they had so many kids," said Pauline.

People describe Elva as a beautiful redhead with a great figure and a bubbly personality.

"Elva was Ken's woman, and that was it. When Ken was away, he wasn't thinking about other women. He was thinking about how to make money," said Pauline.

The Leishmans were active in the typical suburban neighbourhood. The family partook in neighbourhood events like block parties and Halloween parties. At a corn roast neighbours held at the sand pits near Birds Hill, Ken supplied the corn.

Cyril recalls the March 4, 1966 snowstorm. Some neighbours came over for dinner Friday evening as the storm was starting to abate. The neighbours had to crawl to get to the Deane house. Then they slid down the Deane's drifted over car into the carport to enter the side door.

The following day, Cyril was out shovelling snow like the rest of southern Manitoba, when Ken Leishman came out to talk to him. The Great Gold Robbery was five days old. None of the neighbours suspected Leishman. "I was shovelling outside. I had loaned Ken some money. He came out and said he'd have the money in a couple days. He said a partner had sold some property."

William Kenneth Leishman was born June 20, 1931, in Treherne, 120 kilometres south and slightly west of Winnipeg. He was of Belgian descent. He was born into a bad marriage. His father didn't come home at night, and his mother re-married several men in quick succession. Ken was moved around to half a dozen foster homes, usually homes of friends or relatives or his grandparents. He quit school at age 14 before finishing Grade 7 and worked at various odd jobs. At 17, while attending a funeral in Somerset, he met a red-haired Scottish girl named Elva Shields. They married a year later.

At the time, Ken was working with his father repairing elevators in Winnipeg. One day while repairing an elevator at Geyer's furniture store, Ken climbed out of the shaft and found the store closed and everyone gone home. So he had the bright idea to phone for a transfer truck, and loaded up a sofa, bed, end-tables, two lamps and a kitchen suite and had them delivered to his apartment. It was January, 1950, a month before his wedding, and he thought he'd surprise Elva. Elva didn't know the furniture was stolen. The theft was so easy that after the wedding Ken went back for more. This time when he called the transfer truck the police showed up instead. Ken was sentenced to nine months in jail. All the furniture was repossessed and Elva ended up a new bride in an empty Winnipeg apartment.

Leishman was released after serving four months. Soon after the birth of his first child, and only daughter, Lee Anne, he got a job as a mechanic repairing farm equipment for a company called Machine Industries. The job required him to drive out to farms to fix equipment and Leishman got the crazy idea to fly to the farms. So he bought a cheap old canvas airplane and took flying lessons. Soon he was landing in farmers' fields with a plane full of farm parts. It created a great sensation across the country. Leishman flew into farms in Saskatchewan and Alberta. However, in fall he was charged for flying without a license and received a suspended sentence.

Meanwhile, Machine Industries closed. Unable to find a regular job anywhere because of his criminal record for the furniture theft, Leishman answered an ad to sell stainless pots and pans. Again, he combined his love of flying with selling, and flew into the same communities where he fixed farm equipment but this time selling cookware. He would land

• Leishman and family visit the Rockies.

CRIMES OF THE CENTURY

As Leishman fled the bank with the bank manager on his heels, a woman entering the bank stuck out her foot and tripped Leishman.

on farmers' fields or on farm roads, which was illegal. He was doing sensationally well.

But the pots and pans company went broke, too. That's when the "Flying Bandit" phase of Leishman's life began. Leishman needed money for his family, which had grown to five children. On Dec. 17, 1957, Leishman travelled by commercial airliner to Toronto. Inside a Toronto-Dominion Bank at the corner of Yonge Street and Albert Avenue, Leishman pretended to be a man of means and asked to see the bank manager. Leishman talked his way into the bank manager's office and asked that the door be closed. Then he pulled out a small .22 caliber handgun. The bank manager wrote out a counter cheque for $10,000, had Leishman sign it, then the manager initialed it. Leishman and the bank manager emerged from the office and headed for the teller's cage. Leishman kibitzed and acted like they were old friends. Leishman cashed the cheque and had the manager walk out onto the streets with him. "C'mon, Al. I'll buy you a coffee," Leishman said, within earshot of the other bank employees.

In the bank manager's office, Leishman had asked the manager about his wife and children, and seemed sincerely interested. He escorted the manager several blocks away from the bank, then shook his hand and wished him luck. At the airport waiting to return home, Leishman mailed the bank manager a Christmas card. "Merry Christmas from another satisfied customer," Leishman wrote inside. The day after he got back to Winnipeg, Leishman bought Elva a mink stole.

In Toronto, the robber of the Toronto-Dominion branch was quickly dubbed the "Gentleman Bandit" for his politeness and good manners.

Rick Smit, a former corrections officer who became friends with Leishman in later years, said Leishman was different from any criminal he'd ever met.

"I've seen literally hundreds of criminals and they're very self-centred. They're very egotistical and they really don't care about other people, they care about themselves and that's it. Ken wasn't like that. Ken actually genuinely cared about other people," said Smit, who now owns and operates the *Red Lake District News* newspaper, in Red Lake, Ontario.

Like with the Winnipeg furniture store, the bank robbery in Toronto went so smoothly that Leishman decided to do it again. Three months later he flew to Toronto by commercial carrier. But this time the bank manager was a former military man who wasn't going to back down. As Leishman fled the bank with the bank manager on his heels, a woman entering the bank stuck out her foot and tripped Leishman. His pursuers piled on top of him. Leishman was back in the slammer and now dubbed the "Flying Bandit." He was sentenced to 12 years in prison, and took up residence at Stony Mountain Penitentiary.

Ken never told Elva the truth about why he was going to Toronto. When the police arrested him for the Toronto bank jobs, Elva cried and cried—and went on welfare to raise five children.

Leishman tried to escape Stony Mountain, failed, then worked at obtaining early parole. He took two high school correspondence courses, joined the prison debating club, refereed hockey and football games, and was thespian in the drama club. He edited the prison newspaper *Mountain Echoes* and wrote most of its contents, including poems. He acted as advocate for other prisoners' grievances. He worked out in the gym. His prison jobs included the kitchen work and prison library.

Three years and eight months into his term, Leishman was paroled on good behaviour, just in time for Christmas, 1961.

Leishman tried selling stainless steel pots and pans again lor local company World Wide Distributors. The selling went well for a while until one day the boss called Leishman's bluff demanding a raise. Former North Kildonan neighbour Kelly Main remembers when Leishman quit his job. Main was going duck hunting near Libau, "an evening shoot" as he put it, and Leishman asked if he could join him. Main said he let Leishman use a spare rifle because Leishman wasn't really a hunter.

"We were on our way out, and Ken says, 'That dam (boss),' he said. 'You know, I told him that if I didn't get a raise, I quit. And dammit, if he didn't accept my resignation. I'm out of a job.'" But Main said Leishman didn't seem too perturbed about it.

Next, Leishman went to work for an outfit called Olgat Corporation, which manufactured cleaning products, but it went out of business, too. Then he went selling Avon-like cosmetics for a company called Exclusive Beauty Care Ltd. that boasted organic products and was perhaps ahead of its time. Again, Leishman combined his flying wizardry with selling, and again the company went belly up.

In winter of 1966, Leishman's finances were getting desperate. Ken and Elva had seven children by then; the oldest, Lee Ann, and six boys. Ken approached neighbours Cyril and Pauline Deane for a loan. Leishman said he couldn't meet his mortgage payment and was in danger of losing the house. Leishman was seeing his middle class dream go down the drain. The Deanes still have his IOU for the $500 they loaned him. That's the same loan that Leishman, the day after the snowstorm, said he had the money to repay.

It isn't known how Leishman knew about the gold shipments that landed at Winnipeg International Airport twice a month from Red Lake in northwestern Ontario. Perhaps it was just something he had filed away in his head for years; then, as his finances eroded, he thought of it more and more. One can imagine, knowing what we know about Leishman today, how much he would have relished the idea of a gold heist. When he fell on hard times, the enticement was too great.

CRIMES OF THE CENTURY

Red Lake is a mining town about 175 kilometres north of the Trans-Canada Highway at Vermilion Bay. Gold from two mines there was flown to Winnipeg by a smaller carrier called Transair, then transferred to an Air Canada plane, which then flew the gold to Ottawa for deposit at the Royal Canadian Mint.

Leishman, a flying buff, would go to the Winnipeg airport and watch the planes, and watch the gold shipment from Red Lake arrive, and take notes. He was surprised there were no hidden cameras or RCMP officers to greet the gold. While loitering in the area, Leishman grabbed a few way bills, the kind that had to be exchanged between cargo crews when they transferred the gold. That's all a party posing as Air Canada crewmen would need to take the gold.

Leishman also wandered into off-limits areas many times and learned that an Air Canada freight truck was always left in the hangar with keys in the ignition.

Leishman met John Berry through his sales work, and then met brothers Richard and Paul Grenkow through Berry. They became part of the team. They were younger than Leishman but free of criminal records, which is what Leishman wanted. It seems Leishman's plan was to pay the three men for services rendered. It is unclear how the gold was to be split, but it was to be held by Leishman.

To pay his "employees," Leishman needed a financial backer. For that he turned to lawyer Harry Backlin. Backlin was originally from Sandy Lake, Manitoba, and had changed his name from Backewich to Backlin to make it in the big city. Backlin and Leishman became friends when Backlin, a law student at the time, toured Stony Mountain as part of a law school debating team. Leishman was part of the prison's debating team.

If there is a tragic turn to this story in terms of who took the greatest fall, it's Backlin. He clearly had more to lose than any of the other accomplices, and did lose more. It isn't known if he had a criminal bent, or if he was a sucker for the charismatic Leishman. Heather Robertson in her book *The Flying Bandit* suggests that Backlin was a somewhat reluctant participant. Backlin may have thought his involvement was far enough removed. He would be away on vacation out of the country during the robbery. Perhaps he thought he could say he was just loaning a friend money.

Backlin would put up money so Leishman could pay the other three gang members and keep possession of the gold. They paid the three partners $4,000 up front and at least $2,000 was owing. But Backlin couldn't come up with the final $2,000. Perhaps he led Leishman to believe he had more money than he did, or perhaps he felt it would look too conspicuous.

Leishman outfitted John Berry and Rick Grenkow to make them look like Air Canada ground crew. To do that he bought white coveralls and navy parkas from Army Navy Surplus, and stenciled Air Canada logos on the parkas. At night, it would be hard to tell that the Air Canada insignias weren't real.

Paul Grenkow, Rick's older brother, had the smallest role. He was stationed in Red Lake for two weeks watching the Transair flights load up. He took note of when gold crates were loaded and how many there were. One security measure between Transair and Air Canada was gold shipments were only announced hours before the deliveries. So Paul Grenkow's job was to alert the others when a gold shipment was aboard.

Paul Grenkow called Winnipeg the evening of March 1, 1966, to say that a larger than normal gold shipment was on the way. Ken, John and Rick then met and had a few beers at the Black Knight beverage room of the Airport Hotel, and left at about 9:30 p.m. John and Rick left together and drove to the Transair building. There they changed into their phony Air Canada uniforms and slipped into the Air Canada hangar. The Air Canada freight truck had the keys in it as Leishman promised. The two men waited for the Transair plane to land and taxi in, and for the cargo dolly to roll up to the plane. Then they drove onto the tarmac.

One of the Transair cargo handlers wondered why the Air Canada crew was there so soon. Rick Grenkow and John Berry claimed there was a rush to fly the gold to Ottawa that night. Another version of the story is that Leishman left a phone message with the real Air Canada cargo crew saying the Transair plane would be late. The next step was the way bill. Berry and Grenkow showed Transair the way bill Leishman had stolen; Leishman had also forged the signature of a senior supervisor at the bottom. A Transair crew looked at the way bill in the dark on a winter night, and didn't see anything unusual. The Transair crew waved Berry and Grenkow along, and even helped load the 12 crates containing ingots into the Air Canada panel truck. About 20 passengers on the Transair flight watched the exchange take place but no one took any notice of the Air Canada crew's faces.

The ingots were from Campbell Red Lake Ltd. and Madsen Red Lake Mines Ltd. and the companies had different size bricks weighing up to 92 pounds each. "You wouldn't believe the density of this stuff. A piece the size of a loaf of bread weighed 92 pounds," Leishman said in an interview with the *Winnipeg Free Press* years later.

Berry and Grenkow then drove off and past the Air Canada hangar and right out through the gates into the Air Canada parking lot. There they stopped next to a white Ford convertible and unloaded the gold into the car. Not far away, Leishman was waiting in his station wagon, the heat blowing and the radio on. Berry and Grenkow then drove up to Leishman's car and transferred the gold again.

Leishman, the tail end of his car dragging, drove to Backlin's house in Riverview where Backlin's mother-in-law was house-sitting while

Leishman outfitted John Berry and Rick Grenkow to make them look like Air Canada ground crew.

WITNESS TO A HANGING

CAPITAL CRIME

Back in those days when judicial authorities, and Canadians generally, believed in officially killing people, the method of execution was hanging.

Only murderers were hanged. And every state executioner was "Mr. Ellis," an assumed name inherited from England's hangman who went by the name of Arthur Ellis. Mr. Ellis, by trade, was rumoured to work at plumbing, driving street cars and various other occupations during the many decades a part-time hangman was on call.

Manitoba's hangings for a while took place at Vaughan Street jail in Winnipeg—some of them outdoors in a courtyard—and later in an execution chamber at Headingley Gaol built in 1930, just west of the city. This was one of the few permanent gallows built in Canada, most were crude structures erected when needed.

The hanging in 1951 of Walter Stoney for the murder on March 11, 1950, of Martha Perrault, 30, mother of six, was the second last in Manitoba before capital punishment in Canada was abolished. The last hanging took place just over a year later. Stoney, a 38-year-old cook in the sleazy National Hotel on north Main near Higgins Avenue, had stabbed the woman 18 times with an ice pick during a drinking session in his room. Then he had stumbled over to the railway track paralleling Higgins Avenue and fallen, or thrown himself, in front of a freight train.

Officialdom, tidy and considerate, nursed the man back to health and then hanged him.

By car and bus the official observers went to the event the night of January 17. Heavy cloud made it darker than usual and light streaming from the jail's front entrance was somehow inviting despite the bars and the sombre reason for their visit. When they grouped inside they spoke with subdued voices. A couple of newsmen, several city policemen and Mounties, members of the coroner's jury, the sheriff's office and jail officials—32 persons in all.

One newsman was afraid he'd be sick when it happened. But he felt anticipation, as well, for a spectacle he had never witnessed before, hopefully never would again.

Shortly before 1 a.m., the group was led through cell areas cleared of inmates and entered the eight-metre-square execution chamber to wait for the condemned man. They stood around the gallows, the rope attached to a mighty wooden beam. No legendary 13 steps to death. Two steps up and onto a platform of thick planks which contained two folding leaves of a trap door. A wooden railing corralled the platform. There was a large lever on the entrance side, close to the trap, a lever much like a railway switch. The room was painted institutional green and white.

They stood and waited. The last faces a doomed man would ever see. On all sides of the gallows, a few feet back. No one stood near the door which separated them from the death cell. A clear path from that door to the steps. Just seconds from 1 a.m.

The door opened and there he was, the murderer, looking like an embarrassed bad boy. He walked—or was suspended—between two giant guards who gripped his arms. He wore dark blue trousers, a light blue shirt open at the neck and grey work socks. Unhealthy greyish complexion, wide-eyed, slight smile, questioning. As he floated along supported by the guards, his eyes scanned the spectators' faces, then rose to the ceiling. Officials always insisted a condemned man wasn't doped—but maybe someone had felt sorry for this one.

Time was slammed into reverse. It had been a long wait and suddenly too much was happening too fast. Seconds after the door opened, the guards and the condemned cook were up on the platform. Stoney's hands were trussed behind his back. A black hood was placed over his head. The noose settled around his neck. Mr. Ellis—dressed in a rumpled, blue serge suit; a squat, bull-necked, shiny-bald man with a French-Canadian accent, almost the twin of a hulking wrestler called "The Angel" popular in those days—was up there now, in a big hurry. He shooshed the guards off the platform, yelled something and less than half a minute after Stoney had entered the room, the executioner yanked the lever.

CLAP!

Powerful springs pulled the trap doors down and under to slam against the surface underneath. Tremendous bang. The cook was gone. The rope, trembling, strained down and out of sight in the room beneath. It was 1:04 a.m.

Something else dropped. Civilized veneer flaked from the watchers. They leapt forward to climb up on the platform. Some used the steps; the rest legged over the guard rail to crowd around the final exit and stare down at the man who was experiencing capital punishment. No one appeared self-conscious about such macabre fascination. This was what they had officially come to see. After a couple of minutes the doctor, who had descended a flight of stairs to the room below, stepped up on a stool beside the suspended man, undid a couple of shirt buttons and placed a stethoscope over his heart. He shook his head, fastened the buttons again, and got down from the stool.

Above, the watchers maintained their vigil. One stood with the toe of his shoe protruding an inch or so over the opening. He stared intently. But not at the hanging man. His toe. Dust. He raised the offensive shoe and shined the toe against his other pant leg.

Below, the doctor repeated this check; and again. Fourth time, 1:14 a.m., he nodded and they cut the body down.

Everyone filed downstairs for the inquest. It had taken 10 minutes before the cook could be declared dead. Stoney's face was suffused pink. His tongue was squeezed out six inches. With a flip of his finger, the doctor put the tongue back in place and pushed the jaw shut. The dead man was anointed on the chest and wrists by a Catholic priest who had been with him from 8 p.m. until the trap was sprung. The inquest was held to ascertain precisely how and when this man had met his death.

As the observers left the room, they could hear a din in the jail. Inmates were making the traditional noise of protest following an execution. It sounded dutiful, something like the noise people make on New Year's Eve.

That was it. Except for the party with Mr. Ellis. They all went down to the basement jail kitchen and helped themselves to coffee, sandwiches, jelly rolls and cake. They stood around listening to Mr. Ellis analyze the hanging. He said, proudly, he had figured the weight and the drop just right.

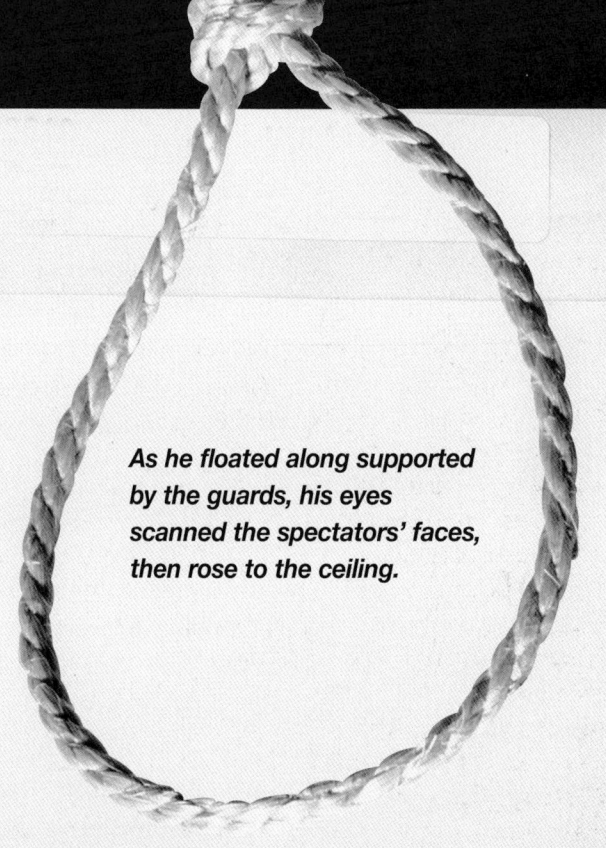

> *As he floated along supported by the guards, his eyes scanned the spectators' faces, then rose to the ceiling.*

CRIMES OF THE CENTURY

It was likely the biggest gold theft in North American history because the truth is gold is just too difficult to steal in large quantities.

Backlin and his wife were on a two-week vacation. Ken told her he was dropping off 11 packages of moose meat in Harry's freezer. She said fine. Ken kept one gold bar for himself. He drove back to his North Kildonan home. At the airport just before midnight, the real Air Canada ground crew came to Transair looking for the gold. The cargo handler's face turned white.

The Air Canada panel truck they found in the parking lot helped explain what happened.

"It was easy," Leishman said later.

Headlines screamed the next day: biggest gold theft in Canadian history. It was likely the biggest gold theft in North American history because the truth is gold is just too difficult to steal in large quantities. There were always people stealing a prospector's stake, or the sporran of gold dust looped to his belt, or workers pilfering dust and nuggets from gold mines. But gold is just too heavy to steal in large quantities. Imagine bricks weighing 90 pounds. Richard Grenkow thought he broke his foot when he dropped one on the ingots during the robbery.

Leishman was on top of the world the next day. People were talking about the Great Gold Robbery from coast to coast. He made his appointment with his parole officer that day and laughed that they couldn't pin this one on him. Of course, with a crime so cool and slick and with so much intelligence—and that involved airplanes—Leishman was the No. 1 suspect from the moment the crime was discovered.

The fast-forwarded version of what happened next goes like this: John Berry phoned Leishman first thing the next morning from the Aqua-Terra Motel where he was staying. They agreed to meet at the Paddlewheel Restaurant after Leishman's parole session. However, for some reason the hotel keeper Joe Krier, who dialed out phone calls so he wouldn't get stuck for long distance charges, listened in on the phone conversation and wrote down the phone number. The men talked in suspicious, code-like language. The phone number provided police with a link between Leishman and Berry.

Later, Berry took a drive out to the Backlin residence and asked Backlin's mother-in-law if he could pick up a pack of moose meat. After all, what's a heist without a little double-crossing? So Berry walked out with one of the crated ingots. That meant Berry had one, Leishman had one, and 10 were sitting in the deep freeze.

Then Leishman turned up March 3rd to reclaim the "moose meat." He planned to stash the gold in a new location in his home town of Treherne but the wind was whipping up and making travel inadvisable. At the same time, he couldn't leave the gold in the freezer or one of his cohorts might pilfer more ingots like Berry did.

So Leishman dropped the ingots in the snow of Backlin's backyard.

Blair Leishman, the fifth child, recalls the next morning. As the snowstorm intensified, he and his three older brothers and their dad walked to the Loblaws store a block-and-a-half away to stock up on groceries. They pulled a couple of toboggans to carry the supplies. "On the way back, we could hardly walk down the street," he said.

"The thing I remember about dad during the storm was him pulling out an encyclopedia and saying we were all moving to Cuba. He was going to buy a small jet and fly rich Americans to Cuba. I remember him explaining we weren't going to get Christmas presents, we were all just going get one small present, because in Cuba you don't get Christmas presents. He was explaining how it was going to be different."

That sounds like something a 10-year-old would remember.

Meantime, Ken borrowed a hacksaw off his neighbours, the Deanes, to cut a six-pound corner off one of the gold bars to show potential buyers in Asia, who could grade its purity. Backlin returned from his vacation and booked a flight to Vancouver, and from there CP Air flight 401 for Hong Kong, to price the gold sample. At the last minute, he would change the plane ticket into Leishman's name.

The police were already on the trail, monitoring Leishman and his associates. Police were also monitoring the passenger lists of people traveling to Vancouver and Asia, and Backlin's name rang a bell with police: his client was Leishman. As well, a doctor surfaced who confessed to back-dating a small-pox vaccination for Ken Leishman so he could enter Hong Kong without the seven-day wait required from the time of the vaccination.

Then Backlin changed his flight reservations into Leishman's name. Backlin was clearly trying to limit his involvement. It was dangerous for Leishman to fly to Hong Kong because it would be a violation of his parole but he had no option.

RCMP were waiting for Leishman and picked him up in the Vancouver airport. Leishman managed to stash the gold sample but was returned to Winnipeg on a parole violation.

Police also spotted Leishman's Cadillac at the Winnipeg airport and shaded in a note pad in the car and found, in the indentation on a blank page, the name "Backlin." That was used to get a search warrant on Backlin.

Two days later police detectives marched into Backlin's office. Police found one of the gold bars in a briefcase beneath the coat rack. It was the one Leishman took. Leishman had delivered it to Backlin and Backlin never bothered to hide it, a carelessness that always baffled Leishman. Backlin told police it belonged to a client and was left without his knowledge or consent. At that point, Backlin thought he might be charged with possession of stolen goods. So while he waited at the police station, Backlin decided to tell all. He wanted to make a deal with police, but they said they couldn't promise him anything. Backlin then suggested police shovel his backyard.

A dozen cops with shovels descended on Backlin's home in Riverview and start throwing snow around. It was like searching for buried treasure. First one crate, then another, then another. They found 10 crates, and the one in Backlin's office made 11.

But the case against Leishman wasn't cinched until RCMP undercover officer Allen Richards, a 15-year veteran on the force, turned in a brilliant jail cell performance as suspected burglar Al Clark. Richards was thrown into a jail cell first with Leishman, then Berry, then the Grenkows. Each one sang like a canary about their exploits in the Great Gold Robbery. Richards goaded them by feigning disbelief that the person he was talking to was capable of such a slick crime. Each one of the robbers, including Leishman, responded by going into greater and greater detail to convince the officer that yes, they were in fact one of the perpetrators of the crime that had the nation's tongues wagging.

Game. Set. Match.

Some of the Leishman clan are ambivalent about their father's exploits, if only because of how their mother suffered. "It set mom a long way back," said Blair.

For example, second oldest child Ron didn't see his father from ages 6-10, when his father was in the pen for his Flying Bandit exploits, and from ages 14-23, when his father served time for the gold robbery. Blair didn't know his father until about age six, and then his dad was back in the pen again from ages 10-18.

After that, his father got out of prison and got a job in Sioux Lookout, where he lived out of a log cabin. Blair stayed back in Winnipeg with his older brothers. "It would have been better if Dad had stayed home and got a good job," said Blair.

Instead of being teased at schools, the Leishman kids had a certain mystique about them. "I think a lot of people admired our dad and thought he was pretty cool. The things dad did were fairly sophisticated. He had a kind of Robin Hood thing about him," said Ron.

The Mormon church, to which the family belonged, was instrumental in helping the family when their father was in prison. The church supplied hampers of food and clothing and a church member let the family live in a house he owned, accepting only the going welfare rate for rent. Elva's side of the family also gave a lot of support. North Kildonan neighbours chipped in with collections of food and other items to help Elva and the kids.

Today, the notoriety of being a Leishman has died down. Blair gets asked maybe three times a year if he's any relation to the Great Gold Robber. None of the seven Leishman children have tried to follow their father's footsteps. None of the children even have criminal records. Two are ex-missionaries with the Mormon church, including Ron, and eldest Lee Ann married a former Mormon missionary. (Members of the Mormon church are asked to do minimum two-year stints of missionary work.) "We've gone totally in the other direction. I wouldn't even think of doing the kind of things my dad did," said Ron.

Ron once asked his dad why he joined the Mormon church. Their father said two Mormons once came to their door to proselytize and he just thought belonging to a church would be a good thing for the family.

Back in prison awaiting trial, Leishman, then 34, did not want to spend the next dozen years or so in the pen. Berry produced the last bar of gold and pleaded guilty, receiving three years. The Grenkow brothers also each received three years, and Backlin was sentenced to seven years. The biggest sentence awaited Leishman. He was already on parole for the earlier bank robberies, and would have to serve that time in addition to any new sentence.

The wheels were turning. Leishman watched for weaknesses in prison security at Headingley Penitentiary for six months while awaiting trial. In September, Leishman and a group of prisoners overpowered 11 guards, took over the prison armory to obtain firearms, and escaped. Only Leishman could have led a motley group of prisoners through the prison security with such precision.

"I've seen lots of high-profile prisoners in my day," said former corrections officer Rick Smit. "I can see that Ken would be able to get his way in the joint. He'd be able to manipulate his way through jail easily. He had the gift of the gab."

"My father was fairly dominant," said Ron, second oldest of the Leishman children. "You knew who was in charge. Even adults knew who was in charge when he was around. He wasn't violent or abusive. But even when he was at Stony Mountain, if my mom said, 'I'll have to tell your father about this,' we would straighten up right away. He just had a firm hand."

Nine men escaped from Headingley. About 50 others milled around but were too close to the end of their sentences to jeopardize their release dates, and stayed behind.

Outside the prison walls, Leishman improvised like mad. He and three other inmates stole a guard's car and barrelled down Manitoba back roads. Leishman planned to reach a small air field at Warren, just north of Winnipeg. There he planned to steal a plane and fly to the United States and possibly all the way to Cuba. The four cons ditched the car and ran as far as the Warren airplane hangar before they noticed the RCMP were waiting there. They took off on foot.

They spent the night in an abandoned farm house. Leishman's next target was St. Andrews airport. This time they hijacked a parked car with a pair of young lovers in it on a dirt road near Warren. Leishman assured the couple they wouldn't be harmed. He only needed the young couple to taxi them to St. Andrews.

Leishman, after all, had never hurt anyone. "A person knew instinctively he wouldn't hurt them," said Smit, the *Red Lake District News* owner. Pauline Deane said when news broke of Leishman's escape, some neighbours suggested

Leishman watched for weaknesses in prison security at Headingley Penitentiary for six months while awaiting trial.

CRIMES OF THE CENTURY

"He just smiled and could talk. He talked himself out of speeding tickets and parking tickets all the time."

he might show up at the Deanes' cabin in Whiteshell Provincial Park and said she should be worried. "I was never worried. Kenny would never do anything to hurt anyone. He was never violent," said Pauline.

The young lovers and convicts arrived at St. Andrews at 3 a.m. Saturday, Sept. 3, and checked the planes on the grounds. But either the planes didn't have gas or didn't have keys. So they all piled back into the car and headed for the airport in Steinbach. They arrived in Steinbach early Saturday morning and hot-wired a small aircraft while other plane owners busied about. The propeller started to turn. Ken thanked the young couple for being model hostages and asked if they'd wait a half hour before reporting them so the convicts could get a good start. Amazingly, the couple did as he asked. In a *Winnipeg Free Press* interview years later, Leishman called them "two really nice kids." Then the plane started climbing the sky and heading south.

RCMP were in touch with U.S. authorities and NORAD but decided against an air chase. Leishman stopped to gas up a few times along the way, then touched down in a cornfield near Gary, Indiana. The plan was to ditch the plane and each convict would go their separate ways. Ken knew someone in Gary who might help them get fake passports. He planned to go to Cuba and get a job flying but needed a passport. Another convict planned to become a merchant marine. But they were wanted men all over the continent by now, making both Canadian and American newscasts with their sensational air escape. Avoiding detection, even in Gary, Indiana, would be difficult. That night, U.S. police stormed their hotel rooms. It was back to the hoosegow.

Leishman escaped again, this time from the Vaughan Street detention centre. He used torn bits of bedclothing to scale a 12-foot fence, severely cutting up his hands on the barbed wire on top of the fence. He was caught later that night. It was a bitterly cold winter night, and he was making a phone call from a phone booth on Main Street when police spotted him. He received a 12-year sentence and served nine.

Elva wrote to Ken daily.

"She wrote a letter to dad every day. Every day," said second oldest child Ron, 50. Each letter was three-to-four pages long. "It was a day by day history for like nine years. She went through what we did every day as a family. If you read the letter you'd be able to tell what I wore to school that day."

Ron asked if he could read the letters but Elva said Ken hadn't kept them.

Leishman's sons say their father was a very charismatic man. "He could sell himself," said Blair. "He just smiled and could talk. He talked himself out of speeding tickets and parking tickets all the time."

What is charisma? Basic psychology describes charisma as a dominant personality but one that is also usually warm and friendly. That doesn't explain Adolf Hitler and Charles Manson but it is variously how we think of charisma today. Psychology says people tend to follow a charismatic person less for the content of the person's arguments, and more for the qualities of the person.

Leishman had charisma, and not just because he took a Dale Carnegie course on How to Make Friends and Influence People while in prison. You don't win over a penitentiary full of prisoners in a matter of weeks, and without having the threat of physical violence against other prisoners, unless you have charisma. People who knew him, including his kids, said he always wore a smile. In almost every picture of Ken Leishman he's wearing that thin, famous smile. "That was dad," said son Ron. Even when he was arrested in Gary, Indiana, their father looks amused. He's smiling, as if it was all a game.

Charisma didn't come from Leishman's looks either. He wasn't bad looking but he was already bald at age 23. He was more of an anti-hairpiece ad.

For centuries, charisma was associated with religion and religious leaders from Jesus Christ to Joseph Smith, founder of the Mormon church. Social scientist Max Weber took charisma out of the religious sphere and brought it down to the level of the lay man. He saw charisma in the whole spectrum of people, ranging from religious leaders, to political leaders, to con artists, and anticipated dangerous charismatic leaders like Hitler and Mussolini. While Weber lived around the time of Karl Marx, his view of society was far more sophisticated. Charisma, to Weber, was "a certain quality of an individual personality by virtue of which he is considered extraordinary and treated as endowed with supernatural, superhuman, or at least specifically exceptional powers or qualities." In other words, the power of the individual.

But even after reading various works on charisma—from the Greek word "kharis" meaning grace or favour—it seems that social science really doesn't know much more than the rest of us. The charismatic person has an abundance of energy, charm, calm, good humour, social skills, and so on and so forth. Each of us can make our own list. Perhaps there's one key trait that person has that makes everything else fall into place. That is, maybe the key is the charismatic person has an abundance of energy and that makes everything else easier. Or maybe the charismatic person has very low-levels of anxiety compared to the rest of us. No one seems to know.

"He wasn't flashy and he never flashed money," said former neighbour Kelly Main. "He was just the most common person you could meet but charming. He'd never say anything against anyone."

"He was a guy with an edge," said Smit, who became good friends with Leishman in

SHOOT-OUT AT THE VIVIAN CORRAL

MAN HUNT

Alexander Zakopiac was born bad to the bone. He started piling up assault convictions before he turned 18, and by age 21 was serving two terms for armed robbery. Albert Proulx was cut from the same cloth, having served ten years for a vicious assault. On Friday July 15, 1952, these two worthies relieved the East Kildonan branch of the Imperial Bank of seven thousand dollars. They were assisted in their efforts by a sawed-off shotgun and two revolvers and were last seen fleeing the scene in a 1950 Oldsmobile.

Needless to say, a massive manhunt ensued, and two days later a report was received of two suspicious looking characters in the vicinity of Vivian, a small town 50 kilometres east of Winnipeg. Several RCMP officers were dispatched to the scene, including Constables John Friend, and George Annand. As they drove down a bush road, they noticed two men walking in their direction. The officers stopped, produced their badges, and questioned the men, who claimed to be locals. Not satisfied with their vague replies, Friend sent Annand for Sergeant Ed Stanley, and Corporal Joe Tessler

As he waited, Friend's suspicions were confirmed when Albert Proulx suddenly jumped him. Friend had the better of it until Zakopiac jammed his .38 into Friend's neck and fired. Annand raced back to find Zakopiac and Proulx trying to get away in the squad car. Friend was nowhere in sight. The three men then began a raging gun battle, which eventually drew reinforcements. Now the lead really started flying. Both fugitives disappeared into the bush, and as the force advanced, they came upon Proulx lying in the grass with a sucking chest wound. He expired as they surrounded him.

Zakopiac made a run for some heavy bush, but Sergeant Stanley brought him down from 120 yards with his old Mauser carbine. Meanwhile, fellow officers had located Constable Friend in a clump of tall grass. They had narrowly missed running over him upon their arrival. Conscious, but in critical condition, he was taken to Deer Lodge Hospital. The bullet had entered the left side of his throat, caromed off his right jawbone, and exited through his right cheek. Amazingly, this trajectory somehow managed to miss his spinal cord and the base of his brain. Friend survived due in large part to the expert treatment he received from a surgeon recently returned from the Korean front.

At trial, Zakopiac conducted his own defence. He received the longest determinate sentence ever handed out in a Manitoba court—30 years.

• Alexander Zakopiac

later years in Red Lake. "He had a lot of dreams and schemes and plans. He was a very interesting, very endearing personality."

What would Leishman have become if raised in a regular middle class family? Probably not a famous gold robber. "He was smart," said Main. "If he'd turned his energies to something straight, he would have gone a long ways."

But blaming Leishman's dysfunctional upbringing for his criminal opportunism has holes, too. His brother Bob, after all, became a policeman with the Winnipeg police force, and is now retired. Bob was not amused by his brother's antics.

Writer Heather Robertson speculates that things may have turned out differently for Leishman except his criminal record kept dogging him. Leishman had landed a good job at Boeing, when Boeing bought the building owned by Machine Industries, the company for which Leishman fixed farm machinery. But then Boeing found out about Leishman's criminal record—stealing the furniture—and let him go. If that hadn't happened, who knows? Coincidentally, Leishman's son Wade, the fourth child, worked at Boeing as of this writing.

Leishman passed his Grade 12 matriculations in prison, and served nine years of his 12-year sentence. He was let out of Stony Mountain in May, 1974. He got a flying job first in Sioux Lookout, Ontario, then in Red Lake. In Red Lake, he was flying air ambulances. Red Lake was the same mining town where the gold came from that Leishman stole.

Leishman was popular there like he was everywhere else. He and Elva and youngest son Trent lived in a house trailer, and Ken built a house boat. Ken was elected president of the Red Lake Chamber of Commerce. He lost a bid to become reeve for the area by 75 votes, but 300 people voted for him.

"Ken was well-received here," said Smit, the local newspaper owner in Red Lake. "He had quite a following. Red Lake is a forgiving place. It almost reveres its outlaw types."

Leishman had no problem with local people promoting the town as "Home of the Flying Bandit." Anything to attract people and capital, he said. The Leishmans ran a local souvenir and clothing store called The Trading Post. Ken would also fly to Aboriginal communities to sell clothes. He loved the North, and told that to everyone he met. He and Elva were finally living happily ever after.

"He seemed pretty satisfied with his lot in life at that time," said Smit. "He seemed to really enjoy life. He wasn't a complainer. He just had a sort of natural, impish charm about him."

On Dec. 14, 1979, Leishman, 48, took his plane, a Piper Aztec, into less than ideal flying weather on a medivac flight between Sandy Lake reserve in Ontario and Thunder Bay. Leishman picked up a woman, Eva Harper, who'd broken her hip on a trap line, and a nurse's assistant, Jackie Meekis. Leishman was working as a relief pilot for Sabourin Airways.

Leishman had no problem with local people promoting the town as "Home of the Flying Bandit."

CRIMES OF THE CENTURY

The plane crash was a severe blow to Elva, who thought at long last she and Ken were settling down together after all they'd been through.

The plane crashed about 45 kilometres northwest of Thunder Bay, in sub-arctic temperatures. Five months later, some fragments of clothing belonging to Leishman and his two passengers were found, but there was nothing left of the bodies. Authorities believe animals had consumed the remains. The federal transportation safety board could not find a mechanical explanation for the crash and suggested it may have been due to pilot error.

Some people speculated that perhaps it was another great Leishman caper to crash the plane and start a new life somewhere, but not people who knew him. "When that plane went down and people speculated he did it on purpose, there wasn't one person in Red Lake who thought that," said Smit. "It would have been so contrary to his personality to kill a nurse and patient. That would never happen."

The Red Lake Museum has a large exhibit devoted to Ken Leishman: newspaper articles, a large collection of photos, even samples from the stolen gold bars. Many people in town are proud to say they were Leishman's friend. He used to hold court down at the Lakeview Restaurant every morning, where locals still go to shoot the breeze.

Ken and Elva's children have turned out remarkably well. Lee Ann, the oldest, now lives in Rexburg, Idaho, and is married to a college teacher. Second oldest Ron is a junior high school teacher in Calgary. He teaches art and graphic art, and also draws cartoons that he sells to advertisers on his Web site: toon-a-day.com.

Third child Dale owns a walnut orchard in California. The three eldest are all participating members in the Mormon Church.

Fourth child Wade is employed at Boeing, and fifth child Blair owns a cow-calf operation near Carman which has about 200 head. He also tried ostrich and emu farming. Sixth child Robert is a wholesale lumber salesman in Winnipeg, and youngest son Trent works for a welding company in southern Manitoba.

The plane crash was a severe blow to Elva, who thought at long last she and Ken were settling down together after all they'd been through. After the crash, Elva moved to California to live with daughter Lee Ann. Elva remarried in the early 1990s, 13 years after Ken's death, to former golf pro Joe Balch. Balch is a former golfer on the Professional Golf Association tour although never a star. He made more money in Pro-Am tournaments, where professional and amateur golfers pair up. Both Elva and Joe are now retired, and like to tour across North America in their motor home. They travel up to Manitoba regularly to see family and friends.

The Leishman children are very happy for their mom, and are fond of their step-dad. "He's a super-nice guy," said Blair. The couple spent over a month in Winnipeg in the summer of 2002.

Meanwhile, Richard Grenkow, one of Leishman's partners in the Great Gold Robbery, took dentistry while in prison and became a dentist. He practised in Winnipeg for almost three decades. He recently sold his dental practice and it isn't known where he is today. Harry Backlin was last reported to be selling real estate in Prince Rupert, British Columbia, but that was back in the 1980s and there is no telephone listing for him there today.

While in prison, Ken Leishman penned a book about his life. Leishman also wrote poetry. When he was released from prison, Hollywood movie star Darren McGavin bought the rights to the book. There was much talk in the papers that a movie was imminent. It was said Leishman might even star in the movie. But the book and movie rights have remained on the shelf and may never get released.

"Dad made a really bad deal," said Blair. "I guess he'd just come out of prison and needed the cash and he went to a producing company who put him onto Darren McGavin. Darren McGavin gave dad $5,000, but said he wanted the book and movie to be released simultaneously. Then Darren got busy with something else and he put it on the shelf and then it got to where Darren thought he was too old to do it." McGavin is now over 80 years old, and Blair believes the rights to the book and movie may never be released.

Son Ron has read the book. It's 600 pages, and recounts the gold robbery in extraordinary detail, as well as Leishman's early life. "He was actually quite a good writer. It's a good read," he said. Ron doesn't have strong feelings one way or the other about it being published, but plans to preserve a manuscript so his kids can read about their grandfather some day.

One final anecdote about Leishman comes courtesy of Cyril and Pauline Deane. It was several weeks after the gold robbery and all kinds of detail about the heist was coming out in the newspaper, including how Leishman had used a hacksaw to saw off the corner of one of the ingots. Some gold dust was even discovered in Leishman's pants cuffs. The six pound hunk of gold Leishman sawed off is the only gold from the Great Gold Robbery never discovered.

Cyril was in the workshop when he called out to Pauline. "Have you seen my hacksaw anywhere?" he yelled. "No," Pauline shouted back. "Don't you remember? You leant it to...." They both started to laugh.

"That Ken was a real sweetheart," said Pauline.

CHAPTER 6

THE MYSTERIOUS MR. KASSER

ALEXANDER KASSER AND THE CFI

Four days after the snowstorm of March 4, 1966, Manitoba Industry Minister Gurney Evans proudly announced a northern mega-project that would see far more money disappear than any gold bars under a pile of melting snow. The dollars that vanished into a pulp and paper mill for The Pas would make Ken Leishman look like a piker. But in the end, the question remains: was this a crime or just shrewd business?

The government announcement was a momentous occasion. Private investors had been found to build a forestry complex at The Pas with the help of low interest government loans. Evans predicted the creation of up to 4,000 jobs, and Manitoba would at long last tap its vast boreal forest. Not only would the forestry complex resurrect the town of The Pas and its region, but it would provide jobs for Manitoba Aboriginal and Métis peoples.

But when the mega-project went off the rails, questions followed, like where did tens of millions of taxpayer dollars go? The provincial justice department would allege fraud of $36.6 million. The mega project, called Churchill Forest Industries, would wind up in courts in Austria and New Jersey, and local civil courts. It would have wound up in Manitoba criminal court had the province's legal efforts been successful. The scandal would include persons and corporations in seven European countries. It would also include Swiss banks where depositors' identities are kept secret; corporations in Lichtenstein, where directors' names can be kept secret; and a company in tax haven, the Bahamas.

CRIMES OF THE CENTURY

Attempts to find investors for a forestry complex in The Pas were stymied again and again over more than a decade.

Churchill Forest Industries would also test the reputations of two of Manitoba's most respected politicians, former premiers Duff Roblin and Ed Schreyer, for the Progressive Conservative and New Democratic parties respectively. The project was initiated by Roblin's government. The Schreyer government would spend most of the money.

Roblin, elected June 16, 1958, explained his rationale for wanting to turn Manitoba's boreal forests into jobs for northerners, in a testimony to a Commission of Inquiry formed in the 1970s to investigate the Churchill Forest Industries (CFI) scandal:

> "We had in Northern Manitoba an immense sub-Arctic forest, called scrub by some, growing, maturing, dying and rotting since the last ice age in a slow 75 to 100 year cycle. It was largely inaccessible, partially unexplored and it had never been fully evaluated...The slow growth cycle produced a long fibre of superior quality for the production of pulp and paper. But the trees were of mixed varieties; they were small and sparse; the stands were far apart; the ground was interlaced with muskeg, streams and lakes; the distances from market were great; communications were few."

Attempts to find investors for a forestry complex in The Pas were stymied again and again over more than a decade. Manitoba government officials shopped around a positive report by Arthur D. Little, an international consulting firm based in Cambridge, Massachusetts, but industry bigwigs saw only marginal profit at best in forestry at The Pas.

A group of investors finally emerged that included Italian, Israeli, Norwegian, British and Canadian interests. But after much effort, investors became worried about the project's viability and backed out.

The Manitoba Development Fund was charged with trying to put a deal together with forestry companies, if possible. The MDF was a Crown corporation formed by the Roblin government. Its mandate was to act independently of government to assist industrial and regional development, mainly as a lender of last resort. The MDF had built up a level of confidence with the government with several large successes bringing new employers to Manitoba.

The province also advertised it was willing to put up as much as $100 million for economic development in primary industries, especially a pulp and paper mill in northern Manitoba. There was still little response, but one company that did come calling was Monoca A.G., a Swiss investment company. In fact, Monoca's enthusiasm was a welcome change from the reluctant investors MDF was accustomed to.

Monoca A.G. proposed setting up Churchill Forest Industries (Manitoba) Limited as a corporation to own and construct a 300-tons-per-day newsprint and/or pulp mill, and a

30-million-board-feet per year sawmill. There would have to be huge government assistance, but the MDF was ready for that. The two sides negotiated that the Manitoba government would loan 86 per cent of the project costs, while Monoca put up just 14 per cent. That is, Monoca would be required to pay $5 million in equity, in order to access $35 million in government loans. CFI would also receive a favourable interest rate of six-and-a-half per cent over a 25-year repayment schedule for the government loans. It would also receive exclusive rights to about one-third of Northern Manitoba forests.

The deal was certainly rich but it was the old, old story: competition between governments. Saskatchewan was also angling for a forestry complex in its north. The Saskatchewan government was initially prepared to offer much more than Manitoba: a loan of 60 per cent of project costs up to $36 million, also a larger reserve of forest, and other incentives and freebies. So Manitoba upped its offer.

One of the key conditions of Monoca's involvement was that it did not want to disclose its investors, even to the government. This wasn't so much a contractual agreement as a verbal request. Dr. Oscar Reiser, president of Monoca and its sole director, claimed it was contrary to Swiss corporate practice to disclose the names of its shareholders.

The Manitoba Development Fund seemed to agree with those terms, at least at first. The Fund had the authority to provide confidentiality to its borrowers. But the unknown investors became an issue overnight, and a great cause of embarrassment to the government. The opposition NDP and *Winnipeg Free Press* hammered the government daily, demanding to know who was building the mega-project. The *Free Press* unearthed Swiss records that showed Monoca had just $12,000 in capital. Did the government know who it was loaning tens of millions of dollars to?

MDF chairman Rex Grose pleaded with Monoca to reveal at least some of its primary investors to take the political heat off. Grose even threatened to cancel the deal. Premier Roblin also made a special written request to company president Reiser. Reiser at times stalled, saying the decision would be put off until the investors' next meeting a few months off. He claimed Swiss law required the unanimous consent of all Monoca investors before that information could be disclosed. At other times, Reiser responded to Grose with almost disdain, claiming secrecy was part of their arrangement.

The Commission of Inquiry that later investigated the CFI scandal concluded Reiser didn't divulge Monoca's investors because there was only one. His name was Dr. Alexander Kasser.

It was always known that Dr. Alexander Kasser was a principal investor in Monoca because of his dominant role in negotiations with the province, but it wasn't known until seven years later that Kasser was its sole owner. That emerged in a review of Kasser companies in 1973 by the U.S. Securities and Exchange Commission. There it was revealed for the first time that Kasser owned most of Monoca's shares, with members of his family owning the rest. And since Monoca owned Churchill Forest Industries in Manitoba, that meant Kasser was the sole owner of CFI.

Meanwhile, a group of companies under the name Technopulp Inc. was to provide expertise for the project. Again, Kasser was sole owner of Technopulp. The Commission of Inquiry would later conclude that Technopulp charged CFI double the normal cost for managerial and supervisory services.

Kasser had Technopulp companies all over the place. There was Technopulp A.G. in Chur, Switzerland, and subsidiaries Technopulp Inc. and Technopulp Machinery with their head offices in Upper Montclair, New Jersey. There were also Technopulp subsidiaries in Spain and Germany.

When Monoca refused to reveal its investors, ie. Kasser, the MDF decided to press on with the forestry complex anyway. If the deal should go wrong, the MDF could always halt financing, or, if the project had gone past the point of no return, it could assume ownership. As well, Monoca had both a favourable reputation and credit rating, and financial reviews like one by Dun and Bradstreet indicated Monoca had the financial wherewithal to locate the $5 million equity payments required.

But CFI was always seeking changes in its agreement, especially in the loan arrangements with the province. For that, they negotiated with Grose. The Commission of Inquiry later stated Grose was outmaneuvered time and again by Churchill Forest Industries. At one point, Grose was set to accept a lucrative job offer from Kasser at the same time he was doling out tens of millions of dollars in loans to the company.

Rex Grose was a star deputy minister with the Manitoba government. He was made chairman of the MDF in 1966 after years as its general manager. Grose's record as a deputy minister was "exemplary" and "his reputation as a doer was first class," Roblin wrote in his memoir *Speaking For Myself*. But Roblin maintained he should have kept a closer eye on what Grose was doing. Roblin said his main concern was the feasibility of the The Pas project. "I had no idea that the risk we were facing was a different one, the misadventures of a principal actor on the stage, Rex Grose. That came as a shock and surprise," Roblin wrote.

Walter C. Newman, of law firm Newman McLean, acted as legal counsel for the Manitoba Development Fund. Two years into the project in the summer of 1968, he and Kasser got into a shouting match. Newman accused CFI of asking for funding concessions that would allow CFI to recycle government funds into the The Pas project as its own equity payments. Kasser shouted that Newman was calling him a thief. The situation blew over but

Grose ended Newman's involvement with the project. The Commission of Inquiry later concluded that CFI did in fact recycle government funds to pay its initial 14 per cent equity share. And every time CFI put up the government's own money as equity, the government matched it with an 86 per cent loan payment.

The turning point in the project came after the demotion of Newman in 1968. CFI convinced Grose that Manitoba's boreal forests could sustain a much larger complex with many more jobs. Plus, a larger project could tap into a federal funding program, the Area Development Agency (ADA) for about $12 million.

The expanded complex would contain four operations: 1) a 100 million board feet per year sawmill, in addition to the 30 million board feet per year CFI sawmill that was being built—cost: $10 million; 2) a 600-ton per day pulp mill for $35 million; 3) a 600-ton per day paper mill for $35 million; and 4) a plant to manufacture machinery for the pulp and paper industry at a cost of $2.5 million.

CFI was to own the smaller sawmill and the pulp mill, as originally planned. A company called River Sawmills Co. (later found by the Commission to be controlled by Kasser) was to build and own the larger sawmill. M. P. Industrial Mills Ltd. (later found to be controlled by Kasser) was to build and own the paper mill, and James Bertram & Sons (Canada) Ltd. (controlled by Kasser) was to build and own the machinery plant.

The total project cost would now be about $85 million. New costs beyond the original $40 million project were to be shared approximately 60 per cent by government, and 40 per cent by Monoca investors. So the province was supposed to put up about $60 million in total loans, and the Monoca investors $25 million in equity.

How Grose won approval for the expanded project has been a topic of much analysis. First, Grose took the plan to the government to see whether more funding was available. Duff Roblin had stepped down to pursue the federal leadership of the Progressive Conservatives and Walter Weir was now premier. Weir and Sidney Spivak, industry minister, confirmed more funds were available if the MDF board decided to proceed with the expanded project.

Grose then went to the Manitoba Development Fund board and said he had obtained the government's approval for the expanded project. In his report to the Manitoba Development Fund board, Grose wrote: "I have submitted this overall plan to the government for approval and have been instructed to proceed." The board took that to mean the government had approved the expanded project and there was no need for the board to perform due diligence and review it.

"In fact, (Grose) had not been instructed to proceed," the Commission of Inquiry concluded.

...the province was supposed to put up about $60 million in total loans, and the Monoca investors $25 million in equity.

"The payments without invoices or proper supporting documenta-tion...was a clear violation of his duty to protect the interests of the Fund, and hence the trust money which he was handling..."

The Commission of Inquiry portrayed Grose as a bureaucrat fallen into his own personal Hades in his obsession to see The Pas complex completed. The Commission claimed Grose "became personally committed to a pulp and paper project for the North and would allow nothing to stand in the way." Later, it stated: "Grose was so completely convinced of the feasibility of the project that he took any challenge personally."

But Grose's biggest mistake was deciding to advance money to CFI for working capital, instead of requiring supporting invoices first. That opened the faucets from the government treasury. Manitoba tax dollars started to pour into the project: $2 million here, $3 million there, then $8 million, on a weekly basis. The MDF also waived the requirement that CFI obtain at least three bidders for each contract. That did away with any pretense that the companies involved, either owned or controlled by Alexander Kasser, were operating at arm's length from each other. At the height of construction, there were more CFI-related companies draining tax dollars out of Manitoba than spigots in a maple grove during maple sugar season.

The Manitoba Development Fund had hired Arthur D. Little Inc. of Massachusetts as watchdog of funds transferred to CFI. Arthur D. Little became the certifying agent for all moneys transferred to the forestry project's investors. But the consulting firm claimed it never saw any fees or costs out of the ordinary. Some of the Commission of Inquiry's harshest criticism was directed at Arthur D. Little, calling the consulting firm "totally irresponsible and negligent."

The Commission of Inquiry said of Grose: "The payments without invoices or proper supporting documentation...was a clear violation of his duty to protect the interests of the Fund, and hence the trust money which he was handling. His failure to disclose to the Board of Directors of the Fund and to the government the problems with CFI and Kasser and the deviations from Fund policy... was inexcusable."

Also unknown at the time was that Grose had entered into negotiations to take a lucrative job offer from the CFI group. Grose had negotiated with one of the firms involved with CFI called M. P. Industrial Mills Ltd., controlled by Kasser, to become general manager of its paper mill starting Dec. 1, 1969. The contract was executed between June 30 and July 2, 1969. Grose was to become president and general manager of the paper mill for a term of 15 years with a minimum salary of $50,000 per year. If for any reason his employment was terminated, he would be retained as a consultant for life for $25,000 per year minimum.

The Commission called his negotiation for a job a complete conflict of interest for someone charged with dispersing funds to the CFI project. It added that Grose conducted the job negotiations without divulging the fact to government or the MDF board. The Commission openly wondered how that may have impacted the flow of money to CFI.

Grose eventually decided not to take the job for undisclosed reasons.

The Commission of Inquiry's most damning comments were reserved for Kasser.

Alexander Kasser was born in Hungary in 1904. He claimed to have attended the University of Grenoble, and helped pay his way by playing soccer for the well-known Peugeot Soccheau Club of France. He also claimed to have earned an engineering degree with a specialty in pulp and paper, and returned to Hungary where he became manager of the largest paper mill in Eastern Europe by age 29. Kasser claimed that in 1944 he organized and co-directed the Swedish Red Cross in Hungary which worked to save hundreds of persecuted Jews and political targets.

Kasser and his family first immigrated to Mexico, and then to New Jersey, where he ran a pulp and paper consulting business and worked in industry research. He was living in Switzerland when the CFI project began. A Dun and Bradstreet report done for the province prior to the CFI project estimated his personal wealth at about $7–$8 million at the time.

The Commission of Inquiry disputed most of the above personal history provided by Kasser. For example, the Commission of Inquiry could find no evidence of Kasser's claim that he once studied at the French universities Sorbonne and Grenoble, or that he helped Jews escape in Hungary during World War Two. It found other inexplicable holes in Kasser's resume to the point that it wondered who Kasser really was. It did not dispute that he was personally rich.

THEFT, THREATS AND THEATRE

Jack Shapira ran Rainbow Stage Theatre profitably for 21 years before it all came crashing down in 1987 with his arrest and conviction for stealing from the company. Shapira, who drove a Rolls Royce and threw famously lavish Rainbow Stage parties, was convicted of misappropriating $387,000 over an eight-year period. He paid back the money and was sentenced to 18 months in prison.

Jack Timlock was Shapira's understudy at Rainbow Stage. He was also the whistleblower who told authorities about discrepancies in Shapira's accounting practices. For example, Shapira took commissions of up to 25 per cent on advertisements in the Rainbow Stage program, and filed expenses related to his Rolls Royce on the theatre's books.

Timlock replaced Shapira as head of Rainbow Stage, and Shapira was subsequently sentenced an additional 16 months in prison for hiring a hit man to cripple Timlock.

The Commission was more certain that Kasser's had bilked the Manitoba government and taxpayers.

"Nearly all the evidence received by the Commission pointed to the fact that Alexander Kasser was not only the central figure in the entire complex, but also the final authority and decision-maker. It was Kasser, therefore, who devised the scheme that was used to allocate contracts, determine the companies that would be established and/or used in the project, allocate responsibility and

THE AXEMAN COMETH

All murders are horrible, but nothing horrifies the public more than an axe-murder. Especially when the victim is a peace-loving young man.

Michael Hurd came to Canada from Nebraska in the late sixties to avoid the draft. He found a home in Winnipeg, and in August, 1973, brought his mother, and his younger brother up to join him. Michael and Allan occasionally worked for Lido Ammazzini at the Town and Country Fruit and Vegetable market, and befriended the Glesby family, who owned the Ballerina Flower Shop next door. Both men were well liked in their West Kildonan neighbourhood.

On the afternoon of November 21, 1973, Michael borrowed an axe and some shovels from Brian, Rose Glesby's son. He wanted to shovel out some space and clear some brush in his back yard at 412 Hartford Avenue.

Later that evening, he and Allan went to the Town and Country to make up some fruit baskets. They had been there about an hour when Ammazzini noticed a man looking into Michael's van. When he asked the man what he was doing, he and another man took off. Hearing this, the Hurd brothers jumped in the van and went after the two men.

Charles Gessner looked at his watch and wondered who in the world could be at the door at this time of night. It was 11 p.m. and someone was pounding on the front door. Gessner opened the door, and was thunderstruck. Alan Hurd stood on the steps, bleeding profusely from a tremendous head wound. They called an ambulance and Allan Hurd was rushed to the hospital. Police attending at the scene soon discovered the body of Michael Hurd, lying face down in the snow a short distance from the house. His head had been nearly split in two.

Allan would later testify that when they left the Town and Country, they came upon two men, later identified as Jack Wayne Bender, and Dwight Douglas Lucas, in the vicinity of Church Avenue. Michael stopped the van and asked the men if one of them had lost the glove that he had found in the van. Lucas responded by producing a gun, and Bender a knife, The two men got in the vehicle and ordered Michael to drive north on Main Street.

Near Lockport, Michael was ordered to turn off at Liss Road, and drive to a Manitoba Hydro shack. The brothers were then forced into the back of the van where their assailants tied their hands behind their backs. They were then taken out of the van and told to lie on their stomachs, face down in the snow.

After a brief discussion with Lucas, Bender went to the van, returned with the axe Michael Hurd had borrowed, and announced that the two men were going to be killed. Although Lucas subsequently told police that he had wielded the axe, Allan Hurd testified that it was Bender who stood over he and his brother, and began hitting them with the axe.

After a series of vicious blows, Bender stopped, and asked the two prostrate brothers if they "were dead yet." Allan lay motionless until Bender and Lucas fled the scene, then staggered to the Gessner home.

Police subsequently identified Bender and Lucas as the prime suspects, and they were quickly tracked down to a Gilbert Street address and arrested. Both men were later convicted of the murder and sentenced to life.

function of all persons and companies, and determine the use and allocation of millions of dollars of cash involved in the process."

It concluded Kasser, by not having any competitive bidding because he owned or controlled all the companies involved, overcharged the province by $33 million, and netted more than $28 million in clear profit.

The Commission unravelled many schemes for how provincial money flowed. For example, starting in March 1969, Kasser arranged for all MDF money for CFI to be cabled immediately to a company called Bertram Verkaufs A.G. (BVAG) in Zurich, Switzerland, which Kasser controlled. BVAG took a fee of 25 1/4 per cent, and the balance was to be available for expenditures on the project. But BVAG would keep only 1.2 per cent of its 25 1/4 per cent fee, and deposit the rest in Swiss bank accounts for various "Anstalts" or establishments in Lichtenstein. Once the money was deposited in favour of the various Anstalts, it would be out of reach of any potential creditors, including the Canadian tax authorities, the Commission of Inquiry maintained.

One of the easiest to follow examples of how money travelled around is the funding for construction of the two sawmills. The contract was awarded without tender to a company called Blue Construction that had been recently incorporated by a James Brown. Blue Construction had an initial capital of $50,000. James Brown had put up $25,000, and the other $25,000 was put up by Kasser as an interest-free loan. The provisions of the interest-free loan gave Kasser the option to buy 50 per cent ownership of Blue Construction for $25,000. This arrangement made it appear that Brown was sole owner of Blue Construction when in fact Kasser had an option to buy 50 per cent.

So Blue Construction obtained the contract to build the sawmills without tender. But Blue Construction never built the sawmills. For that it contracted River Sawmills to do construction. Yet Blue Construction still charged a fee of 24.95 per cent of construction costs, estimated at the time at $10 million, for a fee of nearly $2.5 million. "Blue's activities approached nil," the Commission of Inquiry claimed.

Blue Construction had arranged for River Sawmills to do the construction. But River Sawmills was owned by Blue Construction, and therefore 50 per cent owned by Kasser.

The Commission also unearthed a Bahamas-based company, Montgomery Investment Co. Ltd, that earned about $8.4 million "for doing almost nothing" on the CFI project and, because it was in the Bahamas, paid little or no taxes on its earnings. Again, Kasser had set up the company under another partner's name, but had an option to buy 50 per cent of Montgomery for just $25,000.

One of the biggest losses of funds was the building of a plant to manufacture pulp and paper equipment—one of four components in the forestry complex. Its costs went from an estimated $2.5 million, to $10 million. Yet there was no feasibility study to indicate a market or

"...He was most adept at using other people for his own ends and seeing very clearly how their use would benefit him."

the viability of such a project in The Pas. The manufacturing plant was never in operation for a single day. It never shut down because it never opened.

Excessive fees charged to the Manitoba Development Fund were used by the various companies to pay the 14 per cent equity that private investors were supposed to put up for The Pas project (and later the 40 per cent equity on the expanded project). The Commission of Inquiry estimated the actual equity put into the CFI project by private investors amounted to just $50,000. The rest was recycled government funds.

The Commission concluded CFI overcharged the province by $33 million in excessive fees. The Commission alleged Kasser's methods "involved wholesale misrepresentations, sham corporate entities, the exploitation of respected and prominent personas, and the service of very able professional people, to make the scheme work."

The Commission also alleged that Kasser's plan was meant for "self-enrichment through self-dealing and very high fees" and that "the basic ingredients in its design were anonymity and secretiveness. These elements included non-disclosure and excessive confidentiality."

The Commission said of Kasser: "His competence went beyond the technical—he was able to control people, sometimes because he was respected, sometimes because they found themselves in a position where they thought they needed his help—it is not too strong to say that he was quite capable of ruthless exploitation...He was most adept at using other people for his own ends and seeing very clearly how their use would benefit him."

Kasser never appeared before the Commission of Inquiry. He agreed on two occasions to appear, but backed out.

On June 25, 1969, Manitobans elected the NDP government of Ed Schreyer. The Commission found Grose accelerated the flow of funds to CFI out of concern that the new government might try to take over the project. The NDP had been very critical of the project in opposition. However, the criticism turned out to be largely political rhetoric, and the new government put its complete trust in public servant Grose, just as the previous administration had.

But the outflow of money soon became hard to ignore. During the Conservatives term, only $16.5 million was paid into CFI. From August, 1969, to May, 1970, under Schreyer's watch, $59.7 million was paid out, almost four times as much. The Schreyer government confronted Grose in March, 1970, about the growing expenditures. Schreyer later described Grose as being near tears when questioned about the costs. Grose resigned March 31, 1970.

The NDP government halted funding to CFI in July, 1970. It placed CFI in receivership Jan. 8, 1971.

For all that had gone on before Walter C. Newman published a book telling his version on the CFI affair, one might have expected him to join the chorus condemning Kasser and civil servant Grose. After all, Newman was the lawyer representing the Manitoba Development Fund who was eased out of the CFI project in 1968 because of his frequent clashes over money with Kasser. At one point, he and Kasser had engaged in a shouting match. Kasser maintained Newman was treating him like a thief. Newman shot back that "if the shoe fits, put it on." Kasser said he wanted Newman removed from the CFI project. Grose complied.

On the other hand, the Commission of Inquiry had bashed Newman's name around like it had most individuals associated with the CFI project, including former Premier Duff Roblin. The commission's complaints against Newman resulted in Newman being reviewed by the Manitoba Law Society. At issue was Newman's decision to act as consultant to CFI after he was no longer advising the MDF. The law society cleared Newman of any alleged impropriety.

So it wasn't certain on which side Newman would come down when he self-published his book *What Happened When Dr. Kasser Came To Northern Manitoba*. The name sounds almost like a children's book title, as if Kasser was some Dr. Seuss character dropped into Manitoba's hinterland.

In fact, Newman's book tried to defend who, up to then, had seemed the indefensible: Kasser and Grose. Newman maintained that despite the money schemes of Kasser and the folly of Grose, the forestry complex would never have been built without them.

He pointed out the Manitoba Development Fund created under the Roblin government was a very successful Crown entity, up until the CFI scandal. Among its successes is the J. R. Simplot Company fertilizer plant in Brandon. In almost eight years of operation up to 1966, the MDF made loans to 206 borrowers totaling $44 million without a single loss. It operated at a profit every year, and created, albeit by the government's optimum figures, 3,350 jobs and a payroll of $12 million.

Newman related the many failed attempts of the Manitoba government to interest the forestry industry in a Northern Manitoba pulp and paper mill, even with armfuls of government incentives.

Then along came Kasser. Kasser was "an unconventional genius," according to Newman. "He could and did solve the problem" of creating a viable forestry complex in northern Manitoba. "Ironically, the outstanding innovative features of his design have since gone unrecognized and his remarkable feats of initial construction went for naught," wrote Newman.

Kasser's talent was for "pioneering solutions" in international pulp and paper production. His successes included converting esparto grass in Spain for industrial use, and the processing of North African

• Premier Ed Schreyer

• Premier Duff Roblin

eucalyptus trees, Newman said. Kasser relished the challenge of Canada's North.

"He was a small, explosively energetic man with staring eyes who tended to dominate any group he met," said Newman. "By any standards, he was a genius on an international scale."

Kasser recognized that a Manitoba forestry complex in northern Manitoba needed innovation to be profitable, and he introduced four new concepts for the first time in North America. One of the innovations was a dry debarker that stripped the bark from logs without pre-soaking them. This allowed the dry bark to be used for fuel in wood stoves. His most important innovation was the "flakt dryer" where paper moved forward on a cushion of air shot by nozzles from below. The process allowed the paper to shrink-dry in all directions, helping to produce superior strength.

"Kasser was personally capable of creating or adopting basic design concepts of a pulp and paper mill that would solve technical and cost problems that could deter others," Newman argued.

Kasser also enlisted a top-notch innovator in James M. Brown to develop the complex's sawmill component. Brown had introduced the first automatic sawmill production from undersized logs in the United States.

The problem with Kasser is he didn't want to risk his own money in The Pas project, Newman said. That was where the recycling of Manitoba funds came in. The exorbitant fees, the tax havens, the corporations, many of which were owned wholly or partially by Kasser, were a way for him to move around funds so that he would get 100 per cent financing from Manitoba taxpayers, not just 86 per cent on the first $40 million, and 60 per cent on the second $45 million, said Newman.

That rightly produced the scandal. Newman said that manipulating funds to receive 100 per cent financing does not actually constitute theft because it was loan money, not grant money. Such transactions are sometimes made by machine dealers who charge inflated prices for machinery, after inflating the value of a trade-in. "Neither the buyer or seller are made richer or poorer by the inflated sale price, but the finance company is wrongfully induced to loan unwittingly 100 per cent of its actual value," said Newman. (It should be noted, however, that the capital costs of the CFI project eventually had to be written off.)

The other supposed culprit, Rex Grose, responded to accusations against him in a letter printed in the *Winnipeg Free Press* Nov. 8, 1976. "I have been wrongfully abused in the commission report and my role in it has been most unfairly represented," Grose said. Grose insisted he relied on the expertise of Arthur D. Little Inc. which was hired to ensure that funds were properly managed. Grose said he twice contacted the vice-president of the Massachusetts-based consulting firm to ensure its man on the CFI case, James Zeigler, was performing his function properly, and was assured that he was. "I relied on the experts we retained," Grose wrote from Prince Edward Island, where he had moved to take a job with the provincial government there.

In spring and summer of 1970, a massive construction effort was underway to complete the four forestry projects and start operations by late summer or early fall. Various projects were 80 to 98 per cent completed, with up to 1,600 workers on site. Some of the country's best contractors were there, each with promises from Kasser for large incentives for every day ahead of schedule they completed their part of the project. The construction included such companies as Dominion Bridge, Commonwealth Construction, Honeywell Controls, Otis Elevator, Central Canadian Structures, Taylor Instruments, etc.

Then the government halted funding in July 1970.

When it became known in 1970 that Kasser had maneuvered the project into a position of 100 per cent government financing, it forced the government to take action. But Newman argued the Schreyer government erred when it stopped payments, causing the contractors to walk off the job when the project was almost complete. If CFI had been placed in receivership, as it was later, the work would have been completed for the $7.5 million budgeted for, and the plant would have opened that same year. Bringing in all new contractors to try to pick up where the original builders and designers left the project, saw the remaining costs balloon to $23.5 million. It also caused the project to lose up to $12 million in federal ADA funds, he said, and it delayed opening the complex, costing up to $45 million on gross sales.

The Commission of Inquiry report cost $3.9 million itself and took almost four years to complete.

The Commission's report was criticized by some as a political document. While roundly condemning former premier Roblin, it barely laid a glove on the Schreyer government. It seems more likely the Commission of Inquiry reflected the political ideology of the times. It was the climate in which Petro Canada was formed. In opposition, the NDP had attacked the use of government funds to help private industry exploit the province's natural resources. Pundits argued that the people should own the country's natural resources, not multinational corporations. The NDP would go on to finance money-losing ventures like Flyer Industries (before it was sold into private hands) and Saunders Industries to the tune of over $70 million in the mid 1970s. Government later dealt a serious blow to mining exploration in Manitoba by insisting government get 50 per cent of whatever new ore companies discovered.

The Commission showed a similar ideological stripe when it launched into a lengthy polemic claiming that The Pas did not benefit from having the forestry complex and the jobs that came with it. This seemed somewhat out of place in the whole context of the report. The commission likely reflected public cynicism toward private industry in general in the 1970s.

"The problem with Kasser is he didn't want to risk his own money in The Pas project..."

CRIMES OF THE CENTURY

Kasser took out full page ads in Winnipeg newspapers to claim his innocence.

The three commissioners were former chief justice C. Rhodes Smith; University of Manitoba political science professor Murray S. Donnelly; and labour lawyer and Manitoba municipal board chairman Leon Mitchell. Donnelly showed his colours in a speech blaming the CFI fiasco on the "essentially ideological" view of the Roblin government. Donnelly said CFI should have been a Crown corporation from the outset, and that Roblin's problem was he had no faith in Crown corporations unless they were monopoly positions.

But in the "be careful what you wish for" department, the Pas complex was in fact taken over and run by the provincial government for the first 15 years. It proceeded to lose over $300 million before it was purchased by Repap Enterprises in 1989.

The Commission's estimate of a $28 million profit to Kasser is key to allegations against Kasser.

CFI president Lloyd Hale called the Commission of Inquiry's calculations of Kasser's profits "ridiculous," in a letter to the *Winnipeg Free Press*. Hale said half the $28 million profit by Kasser was recycled to pay the equity; "the other half (was) for services of engineers, managers, supervisors and others without which no complex of this magnitude could ever have been built."

Hale added that businesses frequently use multiple corporations and bank accounts to minimize taxes, including the Canadian government's own Canada Development Corporation, which in the 1970s shifted 9.26 million shares in Texas Gulf Sulphur to the Netherlands to cut its U.S. taxes by two-thirds.

Hale maintained the CFI project was thrown into receivership "on unproven allegations without notice or legal representation." He claimed the Commission of Inquiry was a political lynching.

Also, Monoca A.G. president Oscar Reiser told *Free Press* reporter Vern Fowlie, who appeared unannounced one day on his doorstep in Kreuzlingen, Switzerland, that the Commission set its cost estimates too low, which made Kasser's profit look too high. Reiser showed Fowlie an industrial magazine advertising paper mills for sale similar to CFI. There were three projects listing prices of $80-100 million. The Commission had two forestry firms study the project in The Pas, who estimated the cost should have been in the $50 million range, not $80 million.

Kasser's son, Ivan Michael Kasser, testified later to the U.S. Securities and Exchange Commission that his father was richer before the whole CFI project began.

The one question the Commission didn't answer is whether Kasser succeeded. Did he build a forestry complex that all the other forestry bigwigs said couldn't be done? Would there have been a forestry complex in The Pas without him?

Kasser took out full page ads in Winnipeg newspapers to claim his innocence. He also kept close tabs on The Pas project

CROSSTOWN TRAFFIC

ARMED ROBBERY

On the surface, it was just like any other early November morning in Winnipeg—chilly. A construction crew was working on a building between Smith and Donald streets. Some hunters were relaxing in their camper trailer in an adjacent parking lot, and it was business as usual at the Crosstown Credit Union.

At about 11 o'clock a car slowly made its way down the back lane, and stopped beside the back door of the Credit Union. It was directly across from the construction site and the camper. As it idled, the door flew open, three men burst out and ran towards the car. They had just robbed the Credit Union.

Out of nowhere, several of the construction workers and the men in the camper sprang into action, and within seconds the cold air began to crackle with gunfire. They were actually Winnipeg Police officers in disguise, and acting on a tip, had been staking out the scene for some time.

The bandits tried to shoot their way to the getaway car. One of them was hit, and went down. The other two made it to the car, and the driver gunned it down the lane in a desperate bid to get out of the line of fire. But the police fusillade proved to be too much. The car went out of control and crashed into a wall, ending the drama.

None of the police officers were injured, but all four suspects were taken to hospital with gunshot wounds. It was later reported that two of the robbers were in "guarded" condition, but all survived to take up residence at Stony Mountain.

This 1972 incident featured an exchange of gunfire not seen before, or since, in Winnipeg. While the modern day practice of estimating the number of rounds fired had not yet been adopted, it would have been a considerable amount, because one of the weapons in the police arsenal was a Thompson machine gun. In fact, it marked the last time it was used in action.

• The Thompson sub machine gun was used for the last time by Winnipeg Police during the Crosstown shootout.

Kasser could not travel outside Austria without the threat of being arrested, due to the Manitoba government's legal pursuit.

after his removal. He claimed the complex was a victim of mismanagement by the government.

For example, he scoffed at the NDP's appointment of a lawyer out of its own attorney-general's office, Leifur Hallgrimson, to manage the CFI complex when it became government-run Manfor. What made the lawyer competent to run a pulp and paper mill and sawmill?

"The mill was built to go against the market," Kasser tried to explain to the *Free Press*, but instead the province operated it like other pulp and paper mills. "The experts who did understand it were either fired the night of expropriation or left," Kasser said.

Kasser told the newspaper he did not testify to the commission on advice from his lawyers. "It was quite obvious to me...that (the commission's) interrogation of former premier Roblin and Rex Grose was obviously designed to embarrass public servants whose only offense was to try to improve conditions in northern Manitoba," he said.

In some ways, Kasser brings to mind Winnipeger Jack Shapira. Shapira ran outdoor theatre Rainbow Stage profitably for 21 years until he was forced out. It was discovered in 1987 that he had misappropriated almost $400,000 in funds. Shapira would go to jail, yet no one has had the same success with Rainbow Stage since.

Kasser was like Shapira in that he was a one-man show, a maverick, and perhaps the only one who could put The Pas project together. Yet it's hard to sympathize with Kasser when he claims he did not take excessive profits. He should have tendered bids contracts openly and fairly. His remonstrations that he charged reasonable fees should have been tested in the marketplace.

Lengthy legal attempts to bring Kasser and other principles behind CFI to trial were stymied again and again. The province lost bids in both New Jersey and Austria to try individuals connected with CFI for allegedly defrauding Manitoba taxpayers on $36.6 million. An Austrian court in 1980 refuted the allegation that "Kasser wanted to build an industrial plant which would not be in a position to make loan repayments as of April, 1, 1977."

Kasser was tracked down in Austria, where he had taken out citizenship following the CFI fiasco. Kasser could not travel outside Austria without the threat of being arrested, due to the Manitoba government's legal pursuit. At one point, he was wanted by Interpol in 137 countries. Basically, for a man of international dealings like Kasser, it must have been like being under house arrest.

The province did eventually wrest $9 million out of Kasser and 22 other CFI participants in a civil court settlement in 1979. In 1983, it also obtained a guilty plea for theft over $200 from the CFI principals in provincial court, in exchange for a $1 million fine. The province also wrested a settlement of $3 million in a lawsuit against Arthur D. Little consultants. In total, Manitoba spent $4 million in legal fees.

In 1984, with his legal problems finally behind him, Kasser travelled to New Jersey for the first known time since the fraud charges arose, to see his daughter Mary V. Mochary announce her Republican candidacy for New Jersey state governorship. Mochary told a *Free Press* reporter that she believed in her father's innocence. "From the beginning, I felt it was a political problem," she said.

Alexander Kasser died in 1997 at age 88 in Vienna, Austria. The Pas forestry complex is not his only legacy.

In 1969, Kasser and his wife Elizabeth created the $2.5 million Kasser Art Foundation, dedicated to supporting art, music, dance and other cultural causes. It is still run by his daughter Mary V. Mochary.

In 1997, Kasser was awarded the title "Righteous Among the Nations" by the Holocaust Museum in Yad Vashem in Israel.

In March, 2002, the Kasser family donated to the Montclair university $4 million in their father's name for construction of the Alexander Kasser Theater. The university called Kasser "an international philanthropist, art lover and one-time Montclair resident," in a press release. The award was made by his daughter Mary V. Mochary and by Kasser's son, Ivan Michael Kasser, founder of Holualoa Companies, a real estate investment and management company.

The international recognition only served to deepen the mystery surrounding Kasser in Manitoba.

Meanwhile, The Pas forestry complex has employed about 1,000 people per year on a consistent basis since its inception—about 600 in its facilities and 400 on contract in the bush and in trucking. The facility produces lumber and unbleached Kraft paper for which it has a niche market in things like durable cement bags and dog food bags.

Repap purchased the troubled forestry complex from the province in 1989 for $40 million plus $77 million in preferred shares for which the government could only get payment of $20 million.

In 1997, Repap sold the plant for $47 million to Tolko Industries Ltd. of Vernon, British Columbia, which owns it to this day. The pulp and paper mills and sawmill now go under the name Tolko Manitoba Inc.

Since purchasing the mill, Tolko has invested $125 million to upgrade the facility. In 2001, Tolko paid out $60 million in salary at its sawmill and pulp and paper mill and $53 million to independent cutters in the woods and to truckers. That was an average year. Take that over the complex's 30 years existence, and it's safe to say the forestry complex has pumped about $3.5 billion in direct wages into the northern economy, in today's dollars. More than 60 per cent of its woodcutters are Aboriginal. About 35 per cent of employees in The Pas complex are Aboriginal. The forestry complex is the third largest private employer in Northern Manitoba after Inco in Thompson and Hudson Bay Mining & Smelting in Flin Flon.

The mill, and the missing money, remains part of the legacy of the mysterious Mr. Kasser.

CHAPTER 7

THE CASE OF THE KILLER COPS

BARRY NIELSEN AND JERRY STOLAR

What was Paul Clear like? I asked that question of an old school chum who knew Paul Clear before he disappeared on August 17, 1981.

"He was like us," my friend said.

What was that? "Like us," meant wasting time hanging out. It was in high school in the 1970s because that's when I knew my friend and my friend knew Paul Clear. "Like us," meant dressing in blue jeans, not being overly ambitious and being way too involved in the social sciences outside classes.

We drank but only occasionally smoked pot and weren't really part of that subculture. We were more into sports and argued hockey and football to torturous lengths.

Everyone smiled that smile that knew success was around the corner. We graduated and wondered what now.

Paul Clear, said my friend, would have blended right in. He was good-natured and likable, not someone who got into fights. He didn't smoke. He was of average build, 5'11" and 175 pounds, and better-than-average looking with dark-brown ear-length hair and a thick mustache. He had boxes and boxes of hockey and baseball cards he'd collected, and devoured sports magazines.

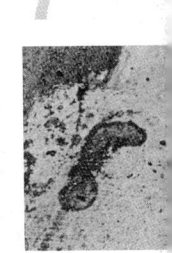

Clear married his high school sweetheart in 1977 after they dated for seven years. He would have been 23 at the time. Everything was still pretty average in his life. The night he disappeared he was planning to get tickets to a Doobie Brothers concert that was coming to Winnipeg. Average. He carried with him a lunch and thermos to work. Average. He was wearing his green work uniform and brown shoes. Average. He and his wife didn't have a lot of money and he drove a 12-year old car that wasn't very reliable. Bonus points. It was a sporty red 1969 Volkswagen coupe, not the beetle kind. More bonus points. His wife called it "a wreck"—huge bonus points—but to her husband it was cool. It had to be started in third gear because the first and second gears didn't work. Off the scale.

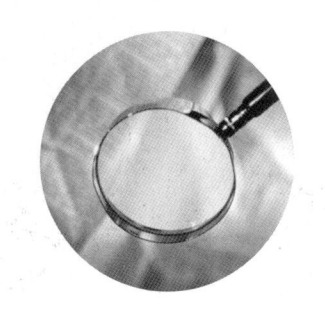

His wife Barbara Clear said her husband Paul was honest and trustworthy. They had a four-month-old son Colin. Barbara Clear was a nurse and planned to return to her job part-time at the Health Sciences Centre, after a six-month leave for the birth of her son.

She said she didn't think her husband had any enemies. "I didn't know anyone who disliked him. He was a friendly person, very outgoing. He had a lot of friends."

Paul Clear was 27 when he was last seen leaving his home at 23 Playgreen Crescent in the Maples. He drove to the Labatt's Brewery on Keewatin Street and Notre Dame Avenue, since closed, to work the midnight shift. His boss phoned his house an hour later to ask why Paul wasn't at work. Barbara didn't know. Paul was never late. She and her brother went out looking, retracing his route to work in case his car had stalled or he'd had an accident.

They found the car parked behind Bun's Master Bakery on Keewatin Street, as if someone was trying to hide it. The next day police found a large pool of blood two kilometres from the Volkswagen in a small turn-in bay on Keewatin at Kinver Avenue. The blood was in the south bound lane Clear would have travelled to get to work. There were also bloody tire tracks from two cars and, oddly, footprints from bare feet. They also found blood on the Volkswagen's right-hand door and on its gas and brake pedals. It looked as if there had been a savage assault, and someone then drove the Volkswagen to the hiding place behind Bun's Master Bakery.

Barbara Clear talked to the press with naive simplicity, and said a day after her husband went missing that she sure he was dead. "I can't understand why anyone would want to hurt Paul," she said. Said Crime Superintendent Herb Stephen: "We have no possible motive in mind whatsoever."

Two days later Winnipeg police reported the pool of blood on Keewatin matched Paul Clear's blood type but they still couldn't find a body. Witnesses driving down Keewatin that time of night claimed to have seen three men talking beside the road, next to two parked cars, one being the Volkswagen.

The story faded off the front pages for a month until a man out berry-picking with his son near Steinbach noticed a peculiar bit of silviculture: a dead tree suspiciously jammed into the ground. The man peered closer and saw that the ground beneath the tree had been disturbed. He summoned police who dug out a decomposed body clad in the green shirt and pants in which Clear was last seen. An autopsy September 10 confirmed that it was

There were also bloody tire tracks from two cars and, oddly, footprints from bare feet.

him. The autopsy showed Clear had been bludgeoned to death, suffering several skull fractures from relentless blows to the head.

The case got tongues wagging, with everyone throwing out a theory about Clear's murder. The *Winnipeg Sun* impugned there may have been another woman. There was an unexplained 11 p.m. phone call to Clear's house by a woman, it reported. On the discovery of the corpse, the tabloid said: "The superintendent refused to confirm whether Clear's wedding ring was found on the body." Exactly what is "refused to confirm" supposed to mean? *The Sun* was suggesting it knew something.

The *Winnipeg Free Press* didn't try to match that theory but some of the actual clues to the mystery were contained in its very first story. The *Free Press* quoted Barbara Clear saying that one of Clear's best friends was a police officer. Several weeks later the newspaper reported that Paul Clear had been interviewed by police a few months before his murder. The *Free Press* said it was around the same time that a close friend, who was a police officer, had been charged with possession of stolen goods. It was the *Free Press* that knew something. Based on their interviews with investigators, police reporters David O'Brien and Gregg Shilliday had uncovered the scandalous information that two police officers were the lead suspects. But after consultations with *Free Press* management and the crime superintendent, the reporters agreed to hold off their "scoop" so as not to jeoparadize the police investigation until charges were laid.

There was a news blackout for the next few months. Then on April 14, 1982, Winnipeg police shocked the city with its announcement that Barry Craig Nielsen, 28, had been arrested for Clear's murder. He was a friend of Clear's. He was also a police constable. Winnipeg police had their man, and it was their man.

Nielsen and Clear weren't really close friends—they were in the same graduating class of 1971-72 after Nielsen flunked a year—but became closer when they married sisters Diana and Barbara Haliuk. Diana was older and married Nielsen. The two young men attended each other's weddings and became brothers-in-law. Nielsen was honorary pallbearer at Clear's funeral.

Nielsen's career was already in ruins before the murder charge. He had been suspended after being convicted for possession of two stolen snowmobiles. He was sentenced to a year in jail but appealed, and was out on bail when police arrested him for murder.

Margaret Haliuk, Diana's and Barbara's mother, defended Nielsen in the media. Nielsen was "a good father. And he is one hell of a fine guy. He got into trouble when he bought some snowmobiles but he didn't steal them." Margaret Haliuk added in her interview with the *Winnipeg Sun*: "I know he didn't do it because he didn't go out that night. My husband was talking to him on the phone."

• Paul Clear

While criminologists used to think the job of police attracted specific personalities, now they are more inclined to think the job shapes the individual.

Three months later a second Winnipeg police officer was charged with Clear's murder. It was as if breakthroughs in the case were metered out at intervals for maximum impact. Police arrested Constable Jerry Carl Stolar, 34, a former partner of Nielsen's with the Fort Garry police division.

Police announced that Stolar and Nielsen were also charged with a break-in at the Manitoba Liquor Control Commission store at 1737 Pembina Highway. Using sledgehammers, they broke into Bunn King Bakeries Ltd. on Pembina, then smashed a common wall with the liquor commission store. They were alleged to have stolen $8,840 worth of liquor.

They were also accused of having cut through a chain link fence of a dealership on Portage Avenue and driven off in a $38,000 Winnebago motor home.

Previous to the murder charge and other theft charges laid July 14, Stolar already faced five charges of possessing stolen property valued at nearly $30,000, including two cars, two snowmobiles, two snowmobile trailers and liquor.

Summing up all the charges for stolen goods came to over $100,000.

Who are police officers? Who becomes a police officer? Sometimes the rowdiest characters you grew up with go on to become cops. "No!" you burst out, when someone you bump into at the supermarket tells you so-and-so became a cop.

"There used to be a theory that people with authoritarian personalities became police officers but research says that's not true," said Doug Skoog, University of Winnipeg criminology professor. "Police tend to come from blue collar families, lower middle class families. They tend to be, although this is less true today, a group of guys that are probably not going to go on to university, and weren't terribly interested in academic stuff when they were in high school."

To these individuals, being a police officer holds a certain allure. "Here's a job that has great security, pays fairly well and is respected in the community. For a blue collar kid whose dad is a plumber or a factory worker, it's a pretty good job," said Skoog. A veteran constable with the Winnipeg Police Service earns a salary in the $60,000 range, before overtime. Police officers can receive full pension after 25 years service.

While criminologists used to think the job of police attracted specific personalities, now they are more inclined to think the job shapes the individual. American sociologist Jerome Skolnick characterizes police as "front-line" workers where individuals at the lowest ranks must make important, street-level decisions. Police academies are not well regarded for preparing someone to be an officer, so the new recruit really learns the job from his co-workers. With the job comes danger and stress. Police tend to suffer from a high level of stress-related illnesses.

DOUBTING THOMAS

COLD FILE

When viewing the Thomas Sophonow case, most of the public attention is focused on the break-down in the justice system that allowed for his wrongful murder conviction. It is all too easy to lose sight of the fact that a young woman had her life brutally snuffed out, and the killer has thus far eluded justice.

Barbara Stoppel was just sixteen when she was strangled and left for dead in the washroom of the Ideal Donut Shop in St. Boniface. The assault took place just two days before Christmas in 1981. She was rushed to the hospital, but her parents were given little hope for her recovery, and five days later she died.

There were several eyewitnesses, including a man named John Doerksen, who claimed to have grappled with the killer on the Norwood Bridge. A composite drawing was released of a thin-faced man, with a mustachio, and wearing a cowboy hat. Police eventually identified Thomas Sophonow, who not only bore a striking resemblance to the drawing, but also just happened to own a cowboy hat, as a prime suspect.

In August 1982, Sophonow was arrested in Vancouver, and charged with the murder. He was returned to Winnipeg, and lodged in the Remand Centre. The police arranged for all the witnesses to view a line-up on March 13, 1982, which included Thomas Sophonow. None of the witnesses, including John Doerksen, identified Sophonow as the man they had seen leaving the donut shop after the murder. Two days later, Doerksen identified Sophonow after seeing him at the Remand Centre.

Based on Doerksen's identification, Sophonow was committed for trial, and the true nightmare began.

At the first trial, Thomas Cheng was called to the stand. He testified that he was in custody at the same time as Sophonow, and that Sophonow had "confessed" to him. Cheng was facing 26 counts of fraud, which were subsequently stayed, but Cheng denied on the stand that his testimony was part of any bargain with the crown. Yet he had told the officer conducting a polygraph test prior to his testimony, that the main reason he was testifying was to have the charges dropped. This admission was never disclosed to Sophonow's defence counsel.

Similarly, there were serious credibility issues regarding Doerksen's testimony that were not disclosed to the defence. So serious, that Mr. Justice Peter Cory, who conducted the inquiry into Sophonow's wrongful conviction, stated that "it is apparent that little, if any, weight can be attached to the evidence of Mr. Doerksen."

There is little doubt that if Sophonow's attorney's had been aware of this withheld evidence that both of these witnesses would have been totally discredited.

As it was, the jury was hung, and a new trial was ordered. Sophonow was convicted at the second trial, but this was overturned on appeal. In 1986, Sophonow was tried a third time, was once again convicted, and once again the Manitoba Appeal Court overturned the conviction. However, this time the Appeal Court took the rare step of directing an acquittal, which was subsequently upheld by the Supreme Court of Canada.

Acquitted. But not necessarily innocent. Thus began the second part of Thomas Sophonow's ordeal. For a lot of people, including some police officers, the Appeal Court's decision did not mean that Sophonow had not murdered Barbara Stoppel, it just meant that he had "got away with it." Fourteen dark years were to pass before this was finally laid to rest. On June 8, 2000, Winnipeg Police announced that, after further investigation, it was certain that Thomas Sophonow was innocent of the murder of Barbara Stoppel.

The press release also contained an apology to Sophonow.

Perhaps the most disturbing aspect of this tragic affair is that within a week of the murder, police identified another suspect that resembled the composite drawing, knew Barbara Stoppel, wore a cowboy hat, lived near the scene of the murder, and did not have an alibi. He was interviewed, and even though police had his prints on file, no one bothered to check them against the prints in the donut shop. The suspect was released.

Police often form a subculture among themselves, and will even buy homes in the same neighbourhoods. There are several clusters of police families living in bedroom communities around Winnipeg like the town of Stonewall.

"One of the reasons historically why police tend to insulate themselves is it has been a male-dominated profession and there's a kind of male camaraderie," said Skoog.

That is changing somewhat with more women joining the police force. While male officers initially resisted the idea of being partnered with a female officer, the women are bringing new qualities to police work. For example, female officers have shown to be a calming influence on violent disputes, particularly domestic disputes.

"The other thing is police are shift workers and don't have ordinary lives," said Skoog. "So they tend to be dependent on each other."

However, the public also pushes police into subcultures. The off-duty officer at a social function can make people uneasy. The public may also hold unfairly high expectations of how the off-duty officer should behave, the way it does for a clergyman, which makes the officer uncomfortable.

"So their recreational pursuits tend to be with other police officers. In their marriages, which frequently don't last, their wives tend to spend time together, too," said Skoog. Police officers can also become isolated from their families, as chronicled by former New York police officer turned criminologist Arthur Niederhoffer, and his wife Elaine Niederhoffer.

"The most difficult adjustment for the wife grows out of the late tour (midnight to 8 a.m.). Every third week she sleeps alone while her husband works the 'graveyard shift,'" the Niederhoffers say in their book, *The Police Family*.

Pessimism slowly sets in as the police officer deals daily with the most base human acts and motives. Niederhoffer maintains police suffer a loss of faith in people. They turn cynical.

"Everybody lies to them," said Skoog. "You talk to cops and they'll tell you they pick up nuns for speeding. Sister Mary Flower Face will look up and say, 'Officer, I wasn't speeding.' And he knows his radar is right. They come not to trust people."

Yet sticking to their own doesn't provide officers with the healthiest perspective of the public. "It's not a particularly good thing because the more insular they become, the more cynical they become, the more removed they become from ordinary day-to-day interaction," said Skoog.

Despite the impression the public may have, corruption in police forces is not prevalent, says Skoog. "If you look at any profession, whether its lawyers, teachers, physicians, newspaper personnel, professors, there's a certain amount of employee theft, a certain number of wife-beaters, a certain number of drunk drivers. I don't think I've ever seen a study anywhere that said rates of corruption are higher in police departments."

However, when police do commit serious transgressions, they are viewed more harshly by the public, and dealt with in kind by the justice system, because police are sworn to uphold the law.

There have been cultures of corruption in some large American city police forces, like New York, Cincinnati and Philadelphia, where large numbers of police officers were found "on the take," but that has never really surfaced in Canada. Corruption in police forces most often happens in narcotics. Police in narcotics have more opportunity for kickbacks.

"Virtually every other kind of policing is reactive," said Skoog. "The public phones and says there's a guy breaking into my garage. With narcotics, for the police department to deal with drugs, it has to be pro-active, that is, they have to intervene in the drug subculture. No one's going to phone them and say, 'Hi, we're smoking some really good dope over here. Why don't you come and arrest us.'

"Because police have to intervene in that culture, it puts them in close contact with people, plus they frequently do undercover work, where they deal with snitches and that puts them in contact where they have to deal with criminals."

But few previous cases of police corruption compares with what Nielsen and Stolar did. There is no pattern among police forces of break-and-enters and selling the stolen goods. Or murder.

"That incident is so out of the ordinary, I don't think it reflected on police culture in any way. I think those guys were just rotten guys. In any profession, you find a certain number of people willing to break the rules," said Skoog.

MURDER ON THE MENU

Winnipeg received a dose of the macabre when Dean Eric Wride murdered his much older wife, then fried up and ate part of her body in July 1996.

The partially eaten body of Esther Johns-Wride, 55, was found in her bath tub in an East Kildonan apartment on Maxwell Place. She'd died from a slashed throat and multiple stab wounds inflicted by her husband of three months, Dean Wride, 33.

Wride testified he was frustrated by the couple's lacklustre sex life.

He kept his wife's dead body in the bathtub for days before mutilating it, cooking and eating a portion.

He laughed when he told one psychiatrist how he stabbed his wife more than 30 times and then went shopping. He also claimed to have used her flesh for fishing bait.

At one point, Wride testified he helped his wife commit suicide so she could get into heaven. He claimed she was suicidal but couldn't enter heaven if she took her own life, so he did it for her.

Neighbours of the Wrides told the *Winnipeg Free Press* they would see Wride walking around in his wife's clothing and wigs.

Several psychiatrists determined Wride suffered from an organic brain disorder. A neurosurgeon testified Wride began to display bizarre behaviour after surgery to repair a burst blood vessel in his brain as a teenager.

"He falls into that dangerous group of people—hyperactive, paranoid and with a great deal of anger," neuropsychologist Dr. Graham Turrall told court. "That makes them highly explosive and highly unpredicatable."

Throughout the trial, Wride "sat in the prisoner's box laughing, mumbling and grimacing," the *Winnipeg Free Press* reported. He grinned twice while the judge found him not criminally responsible of second-degree murder.

He was last reported living in the forensic unit of the Selkirk Mental Health Centre.

The bloody footprint was compared to samples taken from Nielsen. Police had made Nielsen dip his bare feet into a roaster pan of white paint and then walk up and down two 20-foot strips of brown paper.

"It was incredible risk-taking. It was an enormously risky thing."

In the original X-Men comic books, one of the characters is named The Beast. The name stems from his size (400 pounds), strength, and over-sized hands and feet. But mostly he was known for his funky feet, which equipped him with the agility of a circus acrobat to fight super villains. The Beast was one of a few barefoot super heroes, and his feet were nearly as adept as his hands. Of course, it was all due to his mutant birth after his father was accidentally exposed to radiation while working in a nuclear power plant. In comic books, it seems being exposed to radiation is often a plus.

In the pool of blood just off Keewatin Street, *Free Press* photographer Wayne Glowacki remembers photographing the bloody footprint the day after Paul Clear's disappearance. "It was very bizarre. It was this naked footprint stamped in blood. It was an almost perfect print," Glowacki said.

Crown attorney George Dangerfield zeroed in on the footprint. It would mark the first time footprint evidence was used in a Canadian court case.

Dangerfield opened the trial alleging that Nielsen and Stolar had pre-dug a grave for Clear, and then headed him off on his way to work. Dangerfield said the officers planned to take Clear to the grave location 50 kilometres east of Winnipeg to murder him. When Clear resisted, the officers killed him right there on the roadside. Clear's body was found wrapped in a tarpaulin in its burial spot where a berry picker thought the dead tree looked suspicious. Fibers from the tarpaulin were found in Nielsen's car. Stolar's fingerprints were found on Clear's VW bumper. A police sergeant testified it appeared two people dragged the body on Keewatin into a waiting car, including one man in barefeet.

An American anthropologist testified the bare footprint at the murder scene matched that of Nielsen. The bloody footprint was compared to samples taken from Nielsen. Police had made Nielsen dip his bare feet into a roaster pan of white paint and then walk up and down two 20-foot strips of brown paper.

A Scotland Yard identification expert came to the same conclusion, claiming that only one in 60,000 Britons had feet like those at the murder scene: feet with an unusual, almost primate width-versus-length ratio. The Scotland Yard detective pointed to the unusually long first and second toes of the footprint that matched with Nielsen's, and the positioning of the toe stems. He joked that the owner of the bloody footprint would have a hard time finding comfortable shoes.

The defense produced an expert of its own refuting the Crown's experts. Lawyer Hersh Wolch claimed the Crown had spun a fairy tale comparable to Cinderella and the glass slipper. However, one matter that couldn't be refuted was that Nielsen liked to go barefoot. He went everywhere barefoot. One police officer testified Nielsen used to show up at the Public Safety Building in barefeet. Paul Clear's widow Barbara added: "Barry went barefoot quite often. He had slip-on shoes and he hardly wore socks even…He could walk over gravel and it never bothered him." She added Nielsen was proud of his ability to "pick things up with his toes."

The defense strategy, orchestrated by Winnipeg's famous criminal lawyers Greg Brodsky for Stolar and Hersh Wolch for Nielsen, was to bomb the bridges. Brodsky called on Barbara Clear's parents, Margaret and Dan Haliuk, to testify against their own daughter. It seemed a horrific betrayal. It one-upped the worst Greek tragedy: parents siding with the murderer of their daughter's husband.

The parents contradicted their daughter's testimony, and tried to destroy her creditability. They told court she had been acting and talking strangely ever since her husband's murder, as if the jury could not trust her. "They hate me, to put it mildly," Barbara Clear told a reporter at one point during the trial. On one side of the courtroom sat Barbara's parents with their daughter Diana; on the other side sat Barbara Clear and Paul's mother Frances Clear.

It was also like a Greek tragedy in that the trial forced the parents to choose between two daughters. Perhaps the parents simply chose the ground that looked softest. At least one daughter would be happy if Nielsen got off, instead of two daughters suddenly 'widowed'. Expelled from her birth family, Barbara found solace with Paul's mother Frances Clear.

Barbara Clear told a *Free Press* reporter that Paul Clear was the only man she'd gone out with since the age of 16.

"I didn't know what to do (after his death). I just cried a lot. It seemed like my whole life was over." She and Paul were different personalities. "You always knew if he was around. You could hear him laughing or talking. I'm not the outgoing type, so I could hide behind him."

Crown attorney Dangerfield had not yet attended to the motive for Nielsen and wanting to kill Clear. Nielsen and Stolar were charged with running a break-and-enter operation as police officers, and suspended from the force, at the time of Clear's murder. Was Clear involved with them?

Barbara Clear testified she overheard Nielsen call her husband "a fucking rat" at a family gathering. (Her parents testified after her that Nielsen said no such thing. Her mother told court she had no idea why her daughter would say such a thing, and suggested her daughter was out of her mind.) Barbara Clear said Nielsen blamed her husband after Nielsen was charged with possession of stolen snowmobiles, and that her husband felt threatened. "(Paul would) pace up and down. He'd jump to the window if he heard a car coming. He couldn't sleep or eat properly. He'd just never settle down," she said.

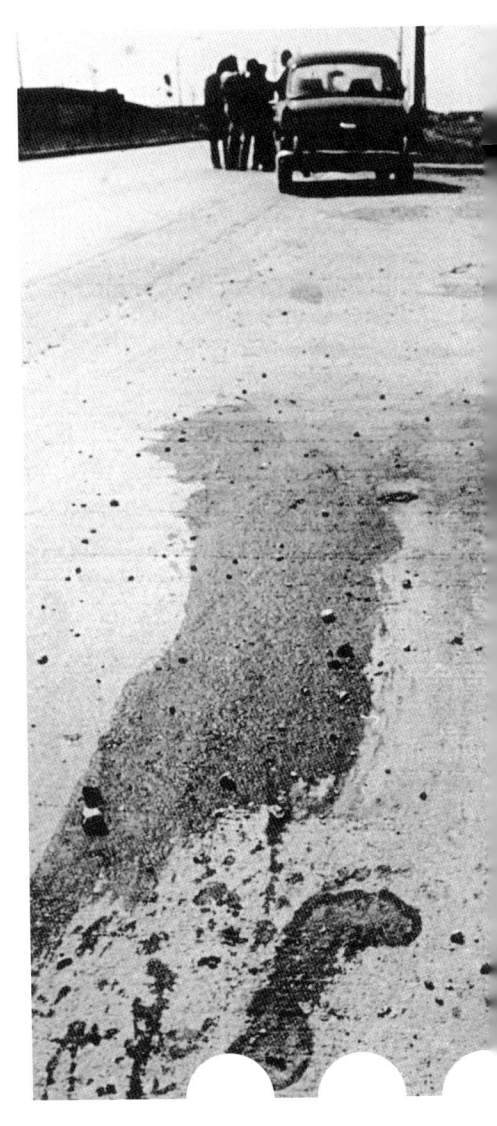

• The bloody footprint that helped convict Nielsen.

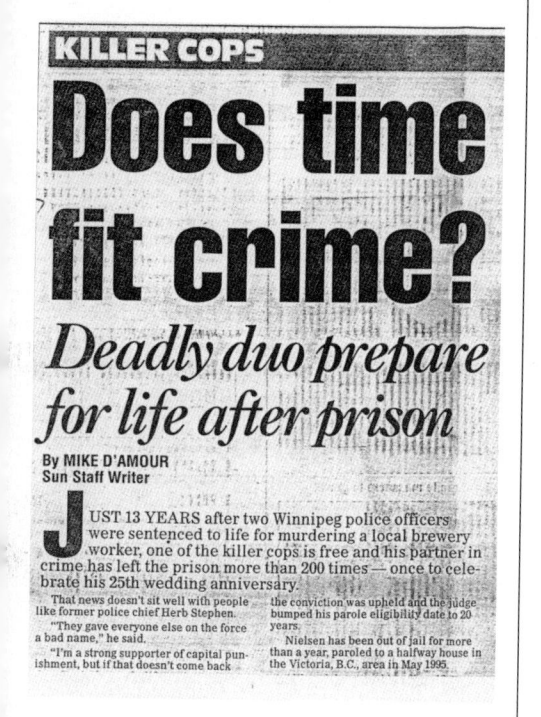

Nielsen telephoned Paul for a private meeting at Vimy Park, which Paul attended reluctantly and returned home "extremely upset. He didn't say much," said Barbara Clear.

In fact, police had taken Clear into custody on April 30, 1981, several months before his murder, on suspicion of possession of stolen goods. Clear was in custody for 10 hours. Police questioned him about some camera equipment in his possession. Clear had obtained cameras from a friend in Calgary, one for himself and one for his mother. Because the equipment was relatively cheap, only $100, Frances Clear checked computer banks in the police bureau where she worked to see if the cameras were stolen. They weren't. Friends at the station liked the camera and Frances asked her son if he could obtain more. Clear was never charged. The friend in Calgary was investigated and found in possession of some stolen tools, not cameras.

The same day Clear was taken in for questioning, Nielsen was arrested for possession of stolen snowmobiles. Nielsen put two and two together: Paul Clear must have finked to police on him.

Detective Sergeant Ronald Morin told court Nielsen got it wrong. Clear never mentioned Nielsen. It was a coincidence. Police were investigating Clear and had tapped his phone. When Paul was picked up for questioning, Barbara Clear phoned her sister Diana Nielsen to see if her police officer husband, Nielsen, could find out what was going on. Diana responded: "I hope they (police) don't come over here." Police listening in wondered why she said that, and appeared at her door soon after to discover stolen goods in their back yard. Police later charged Nielsen with possession of two stolen snowmobiles.

A detective source told *Free Press* reporter David O'Brien that neither Nielsen nor Stolar were part of a internal investigation into stolen property by the police. It was the phone call that led them to Nielsen.

Barbara Clear said her husband didn't even know about the break-and-enter thefts Nielsen was pulling. She had never heard of Stolar until he was charged in connection with Paul's murder. Paul Clear had innocently stumbled into an internal police investigation.

A 12-person jury found Barry Nielsen and Jerry Stolar guilty of second degree murder. Mr. Justice John Scollin ruled they serve a minimum 15 years before being eligible for parole. Stolar still faced an additional 23 property charges and Nielsen faced 12.

The two men appealed and Stolar won a new trial from the Supreme Court of Canada.

In the second trial, Dawnna Donison, mistress to married man Stolar, testified against him. Donison, a psychiatric nurse, said guilt and a new outlook on life persuaded her to come forward and tell the truth. "I can no longer live with the lie knowing what I know," she said.

Donison's new lawyer, Hymie Weinstein, had obtained immunity for her. Donison testified she had also helped Nielsen and Stolar with their break-and-enters, making phone calls intended to divert police away from stores targeted for break-and-entry. Donison said Stolar and Nielsen broke into several Winnipeg businesses in 1980 and 1981 and stole a car, liquor, snowmobiles, microwave ovens, clocks and a mobile home.

Donison claimed she accompanied Nielsen and Stolar at Clear's murder. She was the woman who telephoned the Clear residence just a half hour before Paul Clear left for work the night of his murder. She said it was to see if he was still home. Then she and Stolar and Nielsen drove to Clear's residence and waited for him. Donison said when she asked Stolar where they were going, he said: "We're going to murder Paul Clear."

Donison said Nielsen hid in the back seat that night. They waited about half and hour and then Stolar followed Clear's car. Stolar tricked Clear into pulling over on Keewatin by saying there were sparks coming off Clear's car. Clear and Stolar had never met before. Stolar continued with the charade by looking underneath the VW coupe's chassis. That was how Stolar's fingerprints got onto the bumper of Clear's car, the only evidence linking Stolar to the murder scene up until Donison's testimony.

Donison testified that Nielsen then leaped out of the car and approached Clear. Stolar held Clear's arm while Nielsen struck him in the head with a hammer at least three times. Donison ran off in shock. When she returned, she said she saw Nielsen strangling the still-alive Clear in the back seat of their car.

She said Clear's last words were: "Barry, I didn't do it."

Donison said Stolar warned her not to tell anyone about the murder and that she was an accessory and would suffer the same consequences as them. Donison added that Stolar's lawyer Brodsky also advised her to keep quiet. Brodsky responded in the press saying he only told Donison that she had the right to remain silent. The Law Society of Manitoba later investigated Brodsky's handling of Stolar and Donison, and dismissed professional misconduct allegations against Brodsky.

Stolar's new lawyer Jeff Gindin—Brodsky withdrew from the case when he learned Donison would testify against him—characterized Donison as seeking revenge because Stolar had decided to stay with his wife. "Hell hath no fury like a woman scorned," Gindin said. He also said it was "silly" to believe that Stolar would take her along to witness a murder.

It was the jury that scorned Stolar's defence, finding him guilty a second time. Mr. Justice Michel Monnin added five years to Stolar's sentence for good measure, giving him 20 years without parole.

CHAPTER 8

THE SEARCH FOR ABORIGINAL JUSTICE

HELEN BETTY OSBORNE AND J.J. HARPER

It's been called the Conspiracy of Silence but the silence that greeted Helen Betty Osborne's brutal murder in 1971 went far beyond just a few residents in The Pas.

The real silence was the low self-esteem of Aboriginal people. The real silence was how little political clout they wielded. In 1971, there was no Aboriginal voice. There was no political outcry pressuring the RCMP to commit more resources to catch the murderers of the pretty young Cree girl in The Pas. That was about to change as First Nations people saw what silence brought. They saw that an Aboriginal girl could be raped and murdered and discarded in the snow, and people barely noticed. They saw that their children could be murdered and nothing would be done about it. Silence. Silence of the taiga.

The Aboriginal movement that followed smashed the silence like a pane of glass. The silence surrounding the murder of Helen Betty Osborne helped launch modern day Aboriginal politics, and Aboriginal justice and politics have been inseparable ever since.

All these years later, you just have to look at the high school picture of Helen Betty Osborne. She's pretty, she's casual, she's of her generation. She's starting to feel confident. She has a nice smile but one gets the impression that smile is as wide as it gets. There's someone serious behind the smile. She's a little bit shy but her shyness preserves something genuine that blossoms in the photo.

She felt like an outsider in The Pas because of her race, and found some other native kids to hang out with.

All that was true about Helen Betty Osborne, as documented by Lisa Priest in her book *Conspiracy of Silence*. Osborne was the only student from her grade at Norway House First Nation who was going on to high school. She was going to break the pattern of despair and inertia. School in Norway House ended at Grade 8. So to continue her eduction, Osborne left Norway House to attend a residential school outside The Pas from 1969-71. Then she moved to The Pas to attend public school, and billeted with a local white family.

She wasn't perfect. She felt like an outsider in The Pas because of her race, and found some other native kids to hang out with. By Priest's account, it sounds like she was trying to ditch her goody two shoes image because she had a crush on an Aboriginal guy. The North has a drinking problem, and she had started drinking. She was even thrown in jail a couple times because she was intoxicated. Still, that was more likely to happen to an Aboriginal kid. A white family would have had the means or connections to keep their son or daughter out of the drunk tank.

Her vicious murder in November of 1971 warranted just a three-inch story in Winnipeg newspapers at the time, and then nothing for 13 years. She had been stabbed 52 times. Some brand of white, male, sexual-ego rage had been unleashed on her. She was stabbed in the chest, side and head with a flathead screwdriver.

Look at her picture. The picture is worth a thousand words, and launched 10 million when it finally ran in newspapers 13 years after Osborne's murder. Shame welled up across the country when people saw her picture. She wasn't some woman destined to come to a bad end. Perhaps that's what people automatically assumed at the time of the murder because the victim was Aboriginal. But her picture said otherwise. She was that special child who has the determination to want to rise out of the ruin and rubble of reserve life.

The Conspiracy of Silence was a book title alleging townspeople protected the murderers of Helen Betty Osborne but the argument is tenuous. A conspiracy of silence is when an organization like the military, for example, takes a code of silence to cover up a wrong-doing. The reason for the conspiracy theory is Priest and other media discovered during the trial into Osborne's murder that one of the four men who abducted Osborne had told some other people. It came out as if The Pas was trying to protect her murderers. The truth was the men involved in the murder rotted the air they breathed. They subtracted wherever they went. One was a volatile bully, one would later prove to be an alcoholic and wife-beater, one was a man who spent his life in a drunken fog. Only one of the men was popular in the community.

In fact, the four men were RCMP suspects within months of the murder, and RCMP knew the person, Lee Colgan, who was carelessly making confessions to some people. But RCMP couldn't get Colgan to confess to them, and the people he was confessing to weren't interested in talking to police. The Aboriginal Justice Inquiry, launched largely because of the Osborne murder, also dismissed a racially-motivated conspiracy of silence, saying it was more the case that some people were afraid to get involved.

Helen Betty Osborne was 5'1", 101 pounds. She was the first born child of Justine and Joe Osborne of Norway House First Nation, about 900 kilometres north of Winnipeg. As the oldest child, she was the responsible one and looked after her siblings and dutifully helped her mother with housework. "She was pretty, domestic, traditional, very pleasant, and rarely travelled without her black-beaded rosary," wrote Priest.

"She told me she wanted to become what her family wasn't," a friend of Osborne's told Priest. Wrote Priest: "Betty was unusual in that she seemed to enjoy schoolwork." She liked math. She wanted to finish high school and go to university to become a nurse or teacher or lawyer. She endured taunts from her own reserve for thinking she was better than her peers by going to high school. She had to endure racism and the strangeness of the mostly white environment in The Pas back then. Plus she was older than her Grade 9 classmates because her parents had put her in school late.

She didn't want to go out with white men the way some Aboriginal women wanted to. She thought white men used and mistreated Aboriginal women. It was a political position with her. She wanted to be true to her culture.

On Nov. 12, 1971, Helen Betty Osborne, 19, was out drinking with some friends. She had an Aboriginal boyfriend who was studying to attend Brandon University. That night she ran into her boyfriend in a hotel lobby with another woman. A shouting match ensued between Osborne and the woman, and Osborne stormed out. She stormed out alone, livid in that way of a shy person, her thoughts like capitalized words slamming into each other as she walked briskly away.

Four men happened to be driving down the same street cruising for chicks. The driver was Jim "Smiley" Houghton, 23, who was handsome, a good ol' boy, always grinning, and a bit of a lady's man. He was easy going and the only one of the four that other people actually liked. He would eventually marry his high school sweetheart. He would later become known as the one who got off.

Next to him in the front passenger seat was Norm Manger, 25, a sadsack character who quietly drank himself into oblivion every night. It seemed he never knew what was going on, that night or any other night. He allegedly slept in laundry mats.

The car, a 1967 two-door white Chrysler Newport, belonged to Harold "Bud" Colgan, Manitoba Liquor Control Commission manager for The Pas. His son Lee Colgan, 17, had borrowed it that night. But Lee was too drunk to drive and asked Houghton to take the wheel. Colgan rode in the back seat. He was the one

CRIMES OF THE CENTURY

Osborne ignored the carload but Johnston, presumably to demonstrate the prowess he'd boasted of, would not be ignored.

granted immunity for his testimony in the Osborne murder trial.

The three young men were friends. Somewhere along the line that night they met up with Dwayne Archie Johnston, who was not a friend. Johnston, 18, was a smallish 5'6" but volatile. He tried to make himself seem bigger than he was by frequently getting into brawls and was a member of a local biker gang. He had a reputation for being confrontational and mouthy with police. The Aboriginal Justice Inquiry heard testimony that Johnston "frequently made racist comments to ridicule Aboriginal students in his school classes." Colgan said of Johnston: "I've never seen anybody hate native people so much in my life." Johnston was in the back seat with Colgan.

The carload was loud and boastful and crude. The men were shouting lewd comments about women they'd had or claimed to have had, and were being lewd to insinuate their sexual prowess, which usually insinuated the opposite. They passed liquor around in the white Chrysler. There seemed to be a dynamic of one-upmanship with Johnston in the car. Everyone was trying extra hard to show they wouldn't back down. They were shouting that they wanted to have sex with Aboriginal women. According to Priest, Colgan and Houghton often tried to get Aboriginal women to go to bed with them. They were, in other words, exactly the kind of men Helen Betty Osborne hated.

Osborne likely had her hands jammed in her pockets as she walked down Third Street. She probably clutched a little extra to her dreams of her boyfriend, considering her isolation from home. Those dreams were split open now. She was in no frame of mind to give quarter to anyone, when the car pulled up behind her full of drunken white men making passes at her. Now this, she must have thought. It was turning into the worst night of her life, she must have thought.

Osborne ignored the carload but Johnston, presumably to demonstrate the prowess he'd boasted of, would not be ignored. If he backed down now, if any of them backed down now, all their bullshitting would be revealed for what it was. When Osborne wouldn't stop, Johnston jumped out of the car to persuade her to get inside, his appeal filled with leers and crudeness and alcohol. When she refused, he grabbed her and forced her into the middle of the back seat between himself and Colgan.

This account is from Colgan's testimony years later. The men tried to convince Osborne to have sex with them, Colgan testified. Houghton drove north on #10 to his parent's cottage on Clearwater Lake. They were white, after all, and this was an Indian woman. You could do that. They asked Osborne if she wanted wine, presuming Aboriginal women wanted wine, and when she refused they pushed the bottle into her face. Johnston persisted. He kept arguing with Osborne and shoving the wine bottle at her mouth. Osborne pushed back and he pulled her blouse and tore it. The others laughed and passed the bottle around. Osborne became hysterical and so Colgan grabbed her arms behind her back. Johnston grabbed at her body. She screamed. Colgan said she shouted out: "No white man will ever have sex with me." Houghton kept driving. Osborne broke free her arms and began swinging wildly at Johnston. Colgan cupped a breast from behind and massaged it.

Houghton stopped at his parents' cottage at Clearwater Lake, 30 kilometres outside The Pas, and Johnston took Osborne out of the car and began stripping her. She was screaming. The boys must have been disappointed because she wouldn't stop screaming. So they put her back into the car and Houghton drove to a secluded pump house.

No one would stand up to Johnston. At the pump house, Johnston dragged Osborne outside again and they continued fighting. Houghton also got out of the car, but Colgan couldn't see what part he played. Footprints seemed to indicate two of the men may have been involved, at least to drag her body. Johnston returned to the car to retrieve a screwdriver from under the car seat. A short time after, Johnston and perhaps one of the other men returned to the car without Osborne. Then the four men drove off.

Her ravaged body was found later that day, while the men slept off their hangovers. It was now November 13. Someone had stomped on her face until she was unrecognizable. An autopsy found no evidence of sexual intercourse.

It would be wrong to think RCMP officers at The Pas detachment treated the case lightly because it was an Aboriginal woman. The murder was, in fact, a glory case to whoever solved it. RCMP had enough evidence to search Colgan's vehicle and found eight hairs in the back seat similar to Osborne's. They even found her brassiere strap and metal clasp in the car. They found a screwdriver near the crime scene. But they couldn't prove the four men were with her. A Crown attorney perused the RCMP's evidence and said their case wouldn't get past the preliminary hearing. RCMP followed and harassed the men. RCMP tried

FATAL RECOGNITION

Senseless gang violence reached a peak in Winnipeg in July 20, 1996, when honour student Eric Vargas was fatally gunned down. Vargas was shot eight times. His girlfriend was shot four times but survived.

Vargas and his girlfriend were sitting in a parked car outside Chalmers Community Club in Elmwood at 3 a.m. when youth gang members tried to rob the couple. The gang members started shooting when Vargas's girlfriend recognized one of them. Vargas was six months away from graduating with a degree in economics from the University of Manitoba. He was also vice-president of the Filipino Students Association.

Two gang members were convicted, Robert Bruce Dmytruk and Christopher Leo Ragot, both 20. Dmytruk was convicted of second degree murder and sentenced to life imprisonment. Ragot was found guilty of manslaughter and attempted murder and sentenced to 10 years in jail.

CRIMES OF THE CENTURY

some questionable tactics, like sending over a screwdriver drink (vodka and orange juice) whenever they saw one of the men in a bar. Colgan got actual hand-tool screwdrivers in the mail at Christmas. Town lawyer D'Arcy Bancroft finally fired off a letter to federal justice officials warning the RCMP to back off his clients.

Bancroft knew what had happened because the men told him. He advised them the evidence was circumstantial and told them to keep quiet.

Priest argues RCMP supervisors should have given more direction and more resources to solve the case. They likely would have if Aboriginal people had rallied on the point. But Aboriginal people had little political voice at the time. So the case drifted. Priest claims 200 officers passed through The Pas detachment, each having a look at the huge file that had collected on the Osborne murder. It wasn't until RCMP supervisors put Constable Bob Urbanski on the case full-time in 1984 that things picked up again. RCMP wanted to get the case off their books.

It took Urbanski almost three years to gather enough evidence to lay charges. He used wiretaps on the four suspects' phones, and had listening devices installed in their basements. He ran an advertisement asking for help to solve the crime. It produced little new evidence except for two testimonies.

One was from Gerald Wilson, a court sheriff. A sheriff in Canada is different from the United States. In Canada, he is an officer of the court whose job it is to deliver subpoenas and transport prisoners. Wilson confessed to RCMP that in 1978 or 1979, Colgan had told him about the murder one night in a bar. It was now 1986. Wilson had stayed quiet because he feared getting involved. His reticence sparked outrage, and authorities disciplined Wilson and tried to have him fired but the federal employees' union intervened.

Another key witness to surface was a woman who claimed she'd heard Johnston confess to a murder at a drinking party 13 years earlier. "I picked up the screwdriver and I stabbed her and I stabbed her and I stabbed her," she alleged Johnston said. Her testimony would prove very important.

Urbanski laid a first degree murder charge against Colgan. Speculation is that Urbanski was really trying to scare Colgan into a confession. By this time, Colgan had descended into a life of alcohol and drugs and had even been hospitalized at one point for delirium tremors from alcoholism. Forcing him to dry out in prison could likely prove unbearable for Colgan. Urbanski denied that was his strategy but when he retired recently from the RCMP he said the key to solving "cold" cases was understanding people. He seemed to have understood Colgan.

Colgan's lawyer Don McIver—Bancroft had passed away—was convinced Urbanski was bluffing with his charges against Colgan but wasn't sure how his client would hold up.

Another key witness to surface was a woman who claimed she'd heard Johnston confess to a murder at a drinking party 13 years earlier.

McIver wanted immunity in exchange for Colgan's story. Urbanski knew his case needed it after so many years, and agreed. Colgan's testimony led to Johnston's arrest. Johnston had previously been convicted in 1974 of common assault, and 1981 for firing his rifle in the air to celebrate the American hostages release from Iran.

The trial produced mixed results for the Osborne family and the Aboriginal community. Sixteen years after Osborne's brutal murder, Johnston was convicted of second degree murder and life imprisonment with no eligibility for parole for 10 years. Houghton was also charged with the murder but was acquitted. Manger was never charged. The outcome was not enough for Osborne's family or Manitoba's Aboriginal community. The AJI concluded Houghton should still have been charged with other offenses like abduction, and accessory after the fact to murder. However, the Crown advised the AJI that a conviction was unlikely because the only evidence was Colgan's story, and his testimony wasn't reliable by itself.

Osborne's murder showed what can happen when a race of people have no political voice. When Robert Cross shot native leader J. J. Harper two years after the conviction in the Osborne case, Aboriginal people would not be silent again.

At around midnight on March 8, 1988, a white Dodge Aries was stolen from the parking lot of the Westbrook Hotel on Keewatin Street and Pacific Avenue in Winnipeg by a young Aboriginal male named Melvin Pruden. The car was left running, with the doors locked, and Pruden smashed in the side window and jumped in. He later picked up a friend, who is only named as Allan because he was a young offender at the time, and the pair went joy riding. It was minus 5 celsius outside in the wee

• Const. Robert Cross

CRIMES OF THE CENTURY

• J.J. Harper

hours of March 9, and Winnipeg was slushy from an earlier snowfall.

That was the innocent start to the incident that brought Constable Robert Cross and native leader John Joseph Harper together that night. The truth was both Harper and Cross were in the process of messing up their lives before they met in the dark hours of March 9.

Harper was a smart man. He was a top student all the way through school, even in the residential school where he started. He was from Wasagamack, 400 kilometres northeast of Winnipeg, part of a group of four reserves known as Island Lake. Coincidentally, Cross lived in the Island Lakes subdivision in Winnipeg.

Harper was a former chief of Wasagamack. He resigned, and relocated to Winnipeg to work as executive director of Island Lake Tribal Council and co-manager of the council-owned Nor-Win Construction Company. He was making almost $70,000 a year at the time. He bought a house on Elgin Avenue.

But Harper's marriage was falling apart. His wife Lois was threatening to leave him again. Harper had been abusive and violent with her in the past, and once gave her a black eye.

Harper had been arrested twice under the Intoxicated Persons Detention Act. Both times, Lois had called police. The first incident was on Christmas Day, 1986. Police found Harper drunk and yelling obscenities. He fought with police who had to subdue him with a baton before handcuffing him. On the second incident in late 1987, Harper broke into his former home—he and Lois were estranged—and again fought with police. One officer claimed he drew his gun but then re-holstered it.

Harper was heavily intoxicated the night he ran into Cross. His blood alcohol level at the time of his death in hospital at 3:30 a.m. was .22, almost three times the level of legal impairment for drivers. Two employees of the lounge at the Westbrook said Harper had been acting aggressively that evening. One told the Aboriginal Justice Inquiry that Harper was "spoiling for a fight." The employee said he had to escort Harper out of the bar. Harper left the bar alone and began walking home.

Meanwhile, Constable Cross, 33, was on his second marriage. His wife was pregnant with their third child. Cross wanted her to abort the pregnancy.

Cross had a reputation as a bit of a bully in school. He attended St. Paul's High School and barely scraped by. He also had trouble with the academic side of police school. He was a talkative man, taking after his mother. An article in *Saturday Night Magazine*, penned by someone who knew Cross in high school, said Cross had a temper and was known to be unpredictable. "There's one guy who shouldn't have a gun," one mutual friend said of Cross to the writer Don Gillmor, after the Harper shooting.

Constable Cross and his partner Kathryn Hodgins were from an adjacent precinct near the Westbrook Hotel when the car theft was reported. They joined the search for the car thieves and spotted the car. A chase ensued, a somewhat low speed chase with neither car able to get up to 60 kilometres per hour because of the icy streets. The stolen Airies went through stop signs and traffic lights. Then, heading east on Alexander Avenue, the stolen car veered onto Winks Street, a short spur of a road located between McPhillips and Weston streets, and slammed into a snowbank.

The two thieves were out of the car and running by the time Cross and Hodgins turned

• Hundreds of people turned out for Harper's funeral.

> "Constable Cross had a look in his eyes...The look is he's about to die. I don't know what to say to him. I walk up to him and I start brushing him off. I can't speak..."

the corner. The constables pursued by patrol car, then Cross jumped out and caught the smaller of the two, Allan.

They didn't get a very good look at the second car thief, Pruden. Hodgins estimated him to be native, 22 years old, wearing a dark jacket and blue jeans, and broadcast the description over the police radio. With Allan in the back seat, the constables parked their car in the lane between Alexander and Logan, and listened on the police radio to the search for the second suspect.

At approximately 2:36 a.m., Cross left his patrol car for a look around, and a minute later he heard that a man fitting the description of the second suspect had been arrested. But Cross spotted Harper on Logan, and angled across Logan to intercept him. "I thought to myself, he matches the description, the other one doesn't," Cross said later. Harper was native, wearing jeans and a black jacket, and was in the vicinity of where the car hit the snowbank. However, he was much older than 22, the estimated age of the suspect. He was 36.

Cross asked Harper for identification. Much has been made out of whether Cross had a right to stop Harper. Cross testified Harper said: "No, I don't have to show you nothin'." Cross said that raised his suspicion. Harper brushed past him and Cross reached out to grab Harper. Harper whirled and pushed him. Harper was a good-sized man at six feet tall, 185 pounds and the push knocked Cross over.

As Cross was falling, he pulled Harper down on top of him.

They grappled for a few seconds, then a shot rang out. Harper, shot in the middle of the chest, fell backwards. It was 2:38 a.m. The ensuing autopsy confirmed Harper had been shot at close range.

Whatever his story, fellow police officers arriving on the scene seemed to know immediately that Cross was doomed. Harper was unarmed but he was also native, and there was a new political entity sounding in Canada, the drumbeat of Aboriginal people. Cross's partner Hodgins told the Aboriginal Justice Inquiry: "Constable Cross had a look in his eyes...The look is he's about to die. I don't know what to say to him. I walk up to him and I start brushing him off. I can't speak. 'He jumped me, Kath. I was on my back, on the ground. He went for my gun.' I will never, ever forget what he said, how he said it, and the way he looked."

The Aboriginal Justice Inquiry alleged a closing of ranks among police, starting with Hodgins's claim that she lost some of her notes that night from her interview with the first suspect, Allan. Another officer later was found out to have rewritten and revised his notes. One of the car thieves alleged overhearing an officer tell Cross to say it was an accident, as if he needed that advice. It could have been a cover-up by police but it wasn't that systematic. It could have been mere compassion officers felt for one of their own. It's common for police to believe the public doesn't understand what

KIDNAPPED!

ABDUCTION

One of the most bizarre cases in the history of crime in Manitoba was the abduction of Tammy Wright. Originally from Winnipeg, Tammy had been living in Illinois with her husband Anthony de Silva. A 1987 car accident left her brain-damaged, and de Silva launched a multi-million dollar lawsuit against various parties involved. Although the state of Illinois had named de Silva as Tammy's guardian, Tammy returned to Winnipeg for her medical care, and took up residence at the home of her parents, Ernie and Christina Wright.

The Wrights then brought an application to the courts to obtain custody of Tammy, which, if successful, would give them control over any money awarded to Tammy as a result of the suit. The lure of money often breeds criminal behaviour. In 1992, four men and a nurse burst into the Wright's Mercury Bay home and abducted Tammy in front of her mother.

Alerted by Winnipeg police, U.S. officials stopped the entourage at the border, thwarting the scheme, and Tammy was returned to her parents. The kidnappers included two Chicago police officers, Anthony Lo Bue, and Thomas Kulekowskis, along with de Silva and his father, Albert. All four were eventually charged with Tammy's abduction, but a long series of extradition battles ensued, and the trial did not begin until May 2002.

At the trial, Associate Chief Justice Jeffrey Oliphant laid the blame directly at the feet of Tim Touhy, an Illinois lawyer who had brought the lawsuit, and stood to receive a substantial contingency fee. Justice Oliphant dismissed the perpetrator's contention that they believed their action was legal. Unfortunately, during the long delay, Christina Wright, the only witness to the abduction, had passed away. Unable to proceed with kidnapping charges, the prosecutors accepted a plea bargain. The four men pleaded guilty to forcible confinement, received a two year suspended sentence, and were sent packing back to Illinois.

In the aftermath, the Wrights were awarded custody of Tammy, and Ernie Wright is currently suing the four abductors in civil court. And, undaunted by Justice Oliphant's characterization of his role in the affair, Mr. Touhy is suing Tammy for the contingency fee he would have received.

---

10 WINNIPEG SUN ■ TUESDAY MAY 14 2002

Ex-cops sentenced

But abduction lawyer's idea, judge says

A Chicago lawyer was the mastermind behind the 1992 abduction of a Winnipeg woman, said the judge who sentenced four men involved in the scheme yesterday.

"There is no question at all in my mind that he engineered this whole operation," Associate Chief Justice Jeffrey Oliphant said.

Oliphant said action should be taken against lawyer Tim Touhy in the state of Illinois where he practices.

He made the recommendation after Crown and defence lawyers described a twisted plot to secure a share of a multi-million-dollar settlement the kidnapping victim was expected to receive for a 1987 car accident.

"If I had not been sitting in this courtroom ... I would have thought I was witnessing a tawdry soap opera on television," said Oliphant.

Paralysed, brain damaged

He called Touhy, who was never charged, the "rogue" behind the abduction of Tammy Wright, who was left paralysed and brain damaged by the accident. Court heard Touhy would have received a contingency fee of more than one-third of the settlement.

The four men — Wright's husband, his father and two off-duty Chicago pleaded guilty to

132

it's like to be chasing criminals down dark alleys and not knowing what weapons they carry, while your kids are at home in bed.

There was no dispute it was an accident, just the degree to which it could have been prevented. How much was Cross culpable? There was also no question that there was a struggle. Harper, making a career out of grappling with armed policemen—this was at least the third time he had done it—was living dangerously. Anyone who has had the smallest run in with police knows it's very important for police to see themselves as in charge of the situation. If you interrupt them, or talk about something they don't want to hear, they may get angry. It's no different with reporters or attorneys or judges who can be thrown off when the interviewee or witness turns the tables and asks the questions.

Harper turned and shoved Cross so hard he knocked him down. Police officer Danny Smyth testified at the inquest about seeing Cross moments after the shooting: "He didn't have a hat on. His jacket was on, but done up halfway. There was snow visible on his back, on his top right shoulder, and also snow visible on his right pant leg. His hair looked mussed up."

Losing control of the situation, and having a large man on top of him in the dark, and still in the adrenaline rush from chasing the car thieves, Cross obviously panicked. Cross claimed Harper tugged at his holster while he was on the ground. The gun came out with both Cross's and Harper's hands on it, and it discharged, he said. The make of Cross's .38 calibre revolver had no safety lock on it, which may have been one of the biggest oversights in the entire case.

Cross initially denied pulling the trigger but it became obvious later that he had. And did Harper actually go for the gun, or did Cross simply overreact?

Winnipeg Police Chief Herb Stephen called a press conference just 18 hours after the shooting to announce that an internal review by the police department's Firearms Review Board of Enquiry had cleared Cross of any negligence. The review board had met the same morning of the shooting and concluded it was a result of Harper's attack on Cross. It showed how seriously an attack on a police officer is viewed. You don't push the referee. The haste with which the decision was made, however, did more harm than good. Most people don't think Stephen did Cross any favours by exonerating him so quickly, although there were plenty more hoops Cross would have to go through. An inquest by a chief medical officer awaited, which is mandatory when police officers are involved in a shooting death. The Law Enforcement Review Agency would also review Cross's actions. And a full-blown judicial inquiry was in the offing.

Native leaders were absolutely outraged by Stephen's announcement. Just two years after Osborne's murderer's belated conviction, here was another death of an Aboriginal person

Harper, making a career out of grappling with armed policemen—this was at least the third time he had done it—was living dangerously.

being swept under the rug. Native leaders immediately demanded a public inquiry.

To Aboriginal people, the J.J. Harper shooting was just another example of their mistreatment at the hands of a foreign justice system. They compared Canada to the apartheid in South Africa. More than 500 people rallied on the Legislature steps to demand an inquiry. Attorney General Vic Schroeder took little time to make a decision. He created the Aboriginal Justice Inquiry, appointing judges Mr. Justice Alvin Hamilton of Court of Queens Bench, and Provincial Court Associate Chief Judge Murray Sinclair, to preside.

With three more reviews of the shooting pending, Cross began a slow descent into hell. Actually, it wasn't that slow. Just months after the shooting, Cross and Hodgins were involved in a police car chase and Cross pulled out his revolver and pointed it at the head of one of the suspects. At least that's what he told a neighbour, who was interviewed by Gordon Sinclair for his book, *Cowboys and Indians: The Shooting of J.J. Harper.* "I almost shot another one," he told the neighbours, who were drinking buddies.

Within six months of the Harper shooting, Cross had lost 20 pounds, his wife was in the hospital, and he was looking after three kids. He was suffering constant diarrhea, headaches, and developed a twitch in his eyes "the way spent fluorescent bulbs flicker just before they burn out," wrote Gordon Sinclair. At work, Cross had trouble with memory and mental focus and panic attacks. His right hand shook so badly he couldn't write. He had insomnia and was drinking heavily most days. He was paranoid that Aboriginal people wanted to exact revenge on him. He carried a gun in a plastic bag most places he went, like to the liquor store. Cross's first psychiatrist said he had macho self-image and viewed his emotional problems as weakness. The report by Dr. Linda Loewen said Cross was extremely angry at the native population, his wife and himself.

It was determined he couldn't work anymore after the car chase. He was admitted to the Victoria General Hospital psychiatric ward. He was in tears and suicidal at the time. His wife placed their kids in foster care for the summer. The province's chief forensic psychiatrist examined Cross and reported that Cross "has prominent facial twitches, he stutters, and is quite fidgety. His mood is labile, swinging precipitously from tears to nervous laughter." The report added: "He frequently loses track of thoughts in mid sentence. He cannot touch on certain topics without trembling and breaking down in tears."

Cross was also caught having sex with the married woman next door. His marriage dissolved four years after the shooting. Cross's wife filed for divorce, saying he was unfaithful to her many times.

At the inquest begun April 5, Provincial Court Judge John Enns exonerated Cross.

CRIMES OF THE CENTURY

Dowson didn't order the gun fingerprinted, but his letter suggests his decision was more because he didn't think it would reveal anything as discharged guns rarely show fingerprints.

There were discrepancies in the story but no knockout punch of Cross. It also upheld the basic tenet that you don't go pushing down cops who are in a police chase at 2:30 in the morning. That made the score 2-0 for Cross.

Cross testified again at the Aboriginal Justice Inquiry. A dozen lawyers had standing at the AJI and about half of them had a run at Cross. They cross-examined Cross on how he fell down, where Harper was on top of him, where were Cross's hands when he was falling. They cross-examined Cross as to where his hands and fingers were in relation to the gun's muzzle and trigger, and in relation to Harper as he was falling and grappling with Harper. Several times Cross became confused by the specificity demanded by the lawyers of those few seconds.

Much was made of the lapses in the police's investigation: the gun wasn't fingerprinted (although guns rarely reveal fingerprints, not like on television); Harper's glasses were found by a reporter after police had left the crime scene; several households in the vicinity of the shooting weren't interviewed by police; and police washed down the bloody site of the shooting too quickly.

A second life was claimed when a Staff Sergeant in the Crime Division, Ken Dowson, who headed the department that conducted the investigation, committed suicide the morning he was supposed to appear before the AJI. While he was in charge of the investigation, he was not directly involved until later and took the blame upon himself for mistakes made by his officers. Depression ran in Dowson's family, and he was also known to be a perfectionist. His suicide note said: "The investigation was screwed from the beginning. I've never seen so many things go wrong." He added the poor investigation was a disservice to Cross more than to Harper. He maintained the crime was not racially motivated but no one wanted to hear that. Dowson didn't order the gun fingerprinted, but his letter suggests his decision was more because he didn't think it would reveal anything as discharged guns rarely show fingerprints. "They will never be satisfied until they have their pound of flesh," Dowson said, not specifying the "they." "Maybe God has a place in heaven for cops. Nobody else understands us."

One of the key issues was whether Cross and other police involved in the chase of the car thieves had their guns drawn. The evidence seems to indicate they did. There is no rule stipulating when police can or can't draw their guns. Staff Sgt. Menno Zacharias, who was in charge of training police recruits, did not see anything wrong in Cross having his gun drawn when he approached Harper. Zacharias told the AJI: "The fact that he is a suspect, the fact that a vehicle...had been stolen, there was a chase, people fled the scene and when you're dealing with a potential suspect in a crime you have no knowledge in many cases of whether they are armed, whether they're unarmed, how they're likely to react...My perception of having the gun drawn in this instance might well be having the gun drawn and down at his side, which I don't think is an overly aggressive pose under these circumstances, and in a situation where the scenario runs its normal course, there would be no problem with that."

The AJI commissioners disagreed. They said approaching Harper with gun drawn "is not an acceptable use of police power." The AJI considered recommending that Winnipeg police officers be required to make a report every time a weapon is drawn but declined because "of the tremendous paperwork such reporting would entail."

The AJI hung most of its conclusion on whether or not Cross should have approached Harper. The AJI concluded: "Cross, we believe, got caught up in the excitement of the chase. We believe that he decided to stop and question Harper simply because Harper was a male Aboriginal person in his path. We are unable to find any other reasonable explanation for his being stopped. We do not accept Cross's explanation. It was clearly a retroactive attempt to justify stopping Harper. We believe that Cross had no basis to connect him to any crime in the area and that his refusal or unwillingness to permit Harper to pass freely was, for reasons which we discuss later, racially motivated."

The AJI conclusion leaves plenty of room for contradiction. While the second suspect was apprehended a minute before Cross approached Harper, certainly judges would agree a suspect is what the word implies; the very word suggests the investigation is not over. The AJI conclusion could use an analogy, something perhaps drawn from the judges' legal experience to illustrate why Cross was wrong to approach Harper. From a reporter's bias, the conclusion is simple: you ask. You always ask. To not ask questions of anyone in the vicinity of an event, an accident, a crime gets a verbal slap from an editor. It's surprising what turns up. Information-gathering does not follow a rigid protocol other than to ask questions.

BLOODY HELL IN HEADINGLEY

A blaze lit up the night sky over the RM of Headingley on April 25-26, 1996, in the bloody 24-hour prison riot at Headingley Correctional Institution. A group of gang members at the prison broke out of their cells and went on a drug-crazed rampage. Virtually every window in the three-story prison was smashed before the building itself was set on fire.

The gang members tortured and mutilated guards and many of the 40 sex offenders held in protective custody on the third floor. Gang members tried to carry out a castration of one third-floor inmate, and several inmates had fingers amputated.

"There is blood everywhere," *Winnipeg Free Press* reporter David Kuxhaus wrote while on a tour of the third floor shortly after the riot.

Eight guards and 22 inmates were taken to hospital for treatment. Touchy-feely prison reforms were blamed for the incursion. Prior to the riot, some prison guards had taken to calling Headingley "Disneyland." Damage to the penitentiary was estimated at $2 million.

Rightly or wrongly, the AJI conclusion probably did more good than if it had exonerated Cross, except for Cross.

The question, turned around, may be: would Cross be a slacker, an avoider, a bureaucratic clock-puncher, if he didn't approach Harper, possibly letting the real car thief walk right by him? It may have been the fear that the real suspect could be walking right past him that was Cross's real motivation for stopping Harper. A police officer, like no other job, requires men and women to make split-second, street level decisions. Cross had just four years experience on the force.

That said, what else was the AJI going to find? They were in the midst of hearing about 1,000 testimonies from Aboriginal people about the abuses of the justice system. Was the AJI prejudiced by what it heard? Wouldn't the Harper shooting have simply blurred in with the rest of the tales they heard about police and lawyers taking liberties with the law and constitutional rights?

Whether the gun was drawn was the key question as far as Gordon Sinclair is concerned in *Cowboys and Indians*. Sinclair concludes Cross's gun was drawn, based on the various testimonies and interviews he conducted with people who associated with Cross. Sinclair believes Cross approached Harper with the revolver hidden at his side. There was a salt stain on muzzle which could have indicated the gun touched the ground at some point. With the gun in Cross's hand, and Harper surprising Cross with his belligerence, the situation turned deadly. If the gun hadn't been drawn, Harper might still be alive and Cross might still be a policeman.

Whether Cross was right to have his gun drawn is debatable. The head of police training said he was. Police say they draw their guns because of the unpredictability of their work, and the sudden shove from Harper seems proof of that unpredictability. So after four years of debate and hearings and inquests, and cross-examining those few seconds again and again, the real questions remained unchanged and unanswerable. Why did Cross shoot Harper? Did Harper really go for the holster? Why did Harper shove him? Did Cross panic? What was going through Cross's mind?

The AJI conclusion was a moral victory for Aboriginal people. Rightly or wrongly, the AJI conclusion probably did more good than if it had exonerated Cross, except for Cross. It suggested the system could work for Aboriginal people. It gave Aboriginal people some shield. Police had to be on their guard against abuses or they would be punished. This was demonstrated again in Saskatchewan recently with the "midnight rides" where police, who drove a drunk Aboriginal man out of town and left him there, were punished. Aboriginal people say police have used similar tactics in Manitoba.

Four years after the shooting, the Law Enforcement Review Agency hearings began. Cross didn't appear. He was on antidepressants. Cross's new psychiatrist told LERA: "[Cross] has become the scapegoat of long-standing Canadian problems, current crisis, provincial and city turmoil, televised enquiries, endless litigation, threat of loss of employment, possible imprisonment and threats of injury from community vigilante groups." Cross, in other words, was aptly named.

Dr. Marilyn Mckay added: "Mr. Cross suffers from disabling cognitive deficits. At times it becomes a struggle just to maintain his self-care and carry out small routine activities of daily living."

LERA, in a 3-2 decision, found Cross guilty of using excessive force and abusing his authority. The board ruled that Cross be reduced to rank of fourth-class constable, as if just out of training.

Cross's second wife Diane told Gordon Sinclair: "I always wonder what if it had been Rob who was dead. Probably it wouldn't have been a bid deal. Just like the officer at Oka."

Cross died at age 44 of "acute alcoholism" in March, 1999.

• Inner city gangs are becoming one of Winnipeg's biggest social problems.

An Aboriginal justice system would be less punitive than Canada's justice system, and more of a healing process.

The Aboriginal Justice Inquiry was about more than the Osborne and Harper cases.

Its main conclusions were that government should settle treaties, give first nations self-government, and allow Aboriginal people to have their own parallel justice system. An Aboriginal justice system would be less punitive than Canada's justice system, and more of a healing process. Aboriginal people would create their own laws and justice systems on reserves. It would end the current system of the circuit judges and lawyers parachuting into remote reserves. This process results in interminable delays for those facing charges and/or arrested, and expensive travel costs for all concerned, and the judges and lawyers are unfamiliar with Aboriginal traditions.

The AJI proposal has not been accepted by successive governments. One reason is it could violate the Charter of Rights and Freedoms by creating different laws for different people. There are also other pressing problems for reserves, mainly economic. As well, there is the problem of impartiality when a local Aboriginal judge presides and his second or third cousin stands before him as the accused. The same problem has surfaced with self-government, with nepotism and conflict of interest uncontrolled on many reserves as the 20th Century closed. There have also been many complaints by band members of poor financial record-keeping by chiefs and councils.

In 1988, the Aboriginal gangs started with the Indian Posse and other interchangeable names. Car thefts shot up. Arsons, where most of the arsonists were Aboriginal, blazed through the night. Aboriginal gang members in Headingley Correctional Institution rioted and set the prison on fire. The two provinces with the highest proportion of Aboriginal people, and among the smallest treasuries, Manitoba and Saskatchewan, alternated as child poverty capitals of Canada. People wondered how the social problems would manifest themselves next. Jail cells were disproportionately filled with Aboriginal men and women.

But the late 1990s were also one of the best economic growth spurts of the century, and more Aboriginal people were landing in the work force. Which seemed the under-discussed issue of the century: Aboriginal people and capitalism. Discussions between Aboriginal peoples and the rest of society seem always about government. Yet the dominant force since the arrival of Europeans in North America has been capitalism—the good, the bad, the ugly. It seemed a commission of inquiry might be timely on the relationship between capitalism and Aboriginal people.

And justice and Aboriginal politics were still working in tandem as the century ended. But this time it was justice within first nation governments that was being questioned, a kind of micro-justice, versus the macro-justice where first nations seek redress from the federal government. The micro-justice was the alleged autocratic rule of many chiefs and band councils on their reserves, and how they controlled such things as jobs, housing and education funding. Nepotism was causing first nations to evolve into who-you-know societies, not meritocracies. Aboriginal people were demanding changes. A First Nation Accountability Coalition, comprised mainly of Aboriginal women, sprang up and was outspoken in its criticism of first nation leadership.

In spring of 2002, Ottawa introduced in Parliament proposed comprehensive changes to the Indian Act. The changes would give first nations more latitude to govern themselves but also imposed more financial accountability and disclosure on first nations.

The Canadian government's reasons for taking action was the despairing conditions on many reserves, despite the government's $7 billion annual direct spending on reserves. At the same time, treaty settlements were getting more expensive and not achieving the results hoped for. The spread of capitalism on reserves was also nearly nonexistent. Many reserves have little service industry, even simple services like hair dressers or vehicle or equipment repair shops which circulates money within a community. Instead, money was flying out of the most reserve to obtain those services elsewhere. Unemployment was as high as 90 per cent on reserves.

The *National Post* reported in 2002 that Prime Minister Jean Chretien, who is a former Indian Affairs minister, was personally driving the legislation to revamp the Indian Act. *Post* reporter Luiza Chwialkowska added: "There is an emerging view that the absence of a coherent federal policy with respect to Aboriginal people has created a "policy vacuum" in which courts are led to impose obligations on government. One question is: Will a coherent and "activist" policy backed by significant funds aimed at improving the lot of Aboriginals prevent courts from creating new obligations for government?"

The reporter continued: "While conditions (for Aboriginal people) are improving, the process is thought to be simply too slow to keep up with rapid changes in the economy, especially those that place a higher premium on skills and education than was the case only a few decades ago. As well, the Aboriginal population is growing at nearly twice the rate of the Canadian population, and will become a major part of the labour force of some provinces.

"...In a little-reported speech to Parliament in January, 2002, Chretien declared: 'Quite frankly, I am concerned that, in the case of Aboriginal peoples, we may be spending too much time, energy and money on the past and not nearly enough on what is necessary to ensure a bright future of the children of today and the children of tomorrow. Our approach will be to focus on the future and, most important, on the needs of children.'"

CRIMES OF THE CENTURY

IN THE LINE OF DUTY

Police officers know that every time they go on duty, the possibility exists that they might face a life-threatening situation. Their families live with the knowledge that someday they may have to deal with the unimaginable—that a loved one has been killed in the line of duty.

In the 20th century, the following police officers gave their lives in Manitoba while upholding the solemn oath they took—to serve and protect.

WINNIPEG POLICE SERVICE

Constable Bernard Snowden
APRIL 6, 1918
Shot at the scene of a break and enter.

Sergeant John Verne
JULY 24, 1934
Shot pursuing an armed robber.

Constable Charles Gillis
FEBRUARY 7, 1936
Shot at the scene of an armed robbery.

Constable John MacDonald
FEBRUARY 10, 1940
Shot during a stakeout at a break and enter.

Detective Sergeant James E. Sims
JULY 16, 1950
Shot at the scene of a domestic dispute.

Constable Leonard Shakespeare
JULY 18, 1969
Shot at the scene of an armed robbery.

Detective Ronald Houston
JUNE 27, 1970
Stabbed during a stakeout.

ROYAL CANADIAN MOUNTED POLICE

Sergeant Richard Henry Nicholson
DECEMBER 31, 1928
Killed at Molson, Manitoba while conducting a search for an illicit still.

Constable John George Shaw
OCTOBER 5, 1935
Killed at Benito, Manitoba while transferring robbery suspects to Pelly, Sakatchewan.

Constable Harold Stanley Seigel
SEPTEMBER 26, 1971
Killed while attempting to remove a person from a residence at Iles des Chenes, Manitoba.

Constable Dennis Anthony Onofrey
JANUARY 23, 1978
Killed at Virden, Manitoba while investigating a stolen vehicle report.

Special Constable Robert W. C. Thomas
MARCH 6, 1986
Killed during a routine vehicle check at Powerview, Manitoba.

MANITOBA PROVINCIAL POLICE

Chief Richard Power
JULY 22, 1880
Drowned when a prisoner deliberately overturned a boat on the Red River.

Constable Charles Rooke
JANUARY 26, 1913
Shot near Dauphin, Manitoba while executing a warrant.

Constable James Uttley
NOVEMBER 11, 1920
Shot at St. Boniface during a routine morality investigation.

Constable Alex McCurdy
NOVEMBER 11, 1920
Shot at St. Boniface during a routine morality investigation.

INDEX

A

Aboriginal Justice Inquiry, 124, 125, 128, 129, 131, 134-137, 139
Aboriginal people, 92, 108, 122, 123-127, 131, 133-134, 136-137, 139-140
Aboriginal, 92, 108, 122
Air Canada, 77, 78, 81
Airport Hotel, 69, 78
alcohol, 32-46, 54, 62, 123, 125, 126, 129, 138
Alexander Ave., 130, 131
Altona, 10
Ammazzini, Lido, 99
Anderson, Dan, 69
Anderson, Frank W., 19
Andrews, Const. Jane, 30
Andrews, A. J., 14
Anglican Archdiocese of Rupertland, 56
Anglican, 24
Annand, RCMP Const. George, 87
Arborg, 71
Arbourg, Sam, 45
Area Development Agency, 96, 104
Army Navy Surplus, 78
Arthur D. Little, 93, 97, 103, 107
Assiniboia Downs, 39
Austin, 59
Australia, 19
Austria, 92, 107, 108

B

Backlin, Harry, 77, 78, 81, 82, 83, 84, 90
Bahamas, 92, 100
Balakowski, Ben, 45
Balakowski, Ned, 45
Balch, Joe, 89

Balfour St., 68
Balmoral St., 42
Bancroft, D'Arcy, 127
Bardal, Neil, 45
Belgian, 43, 73
Bender, John Wayne, 99
Berry John, 77, 78, 81, 83, 84
Bertam, Ben (Abramovich), 28
Birds Hill, 73
Birtle, 5
Bishop, Arthur, 65
Blake, Emily Hilda, 1-14
Blow, Wpg. Police Chief George, 68
Boer War, 24
Boissevain, 36, 60
Bond St., 27
bootlegging, 32-46
Boston, 52, 69
Boyd Ave., 33, 39
Brandon 2, 3, 13, 37, 102
Brandon Mental Institution, 12
Brandon Police, 3
Brandon University, 2, 4, 124
Brandon Western Sun, 9
Brazier St., 57
British Columbia, 71, 90, 108
British, 24
Broadway, 51
Brodsky, Greg, 118, 120
Bronfman family, 33, 37, 40, 43
Bronfman, Ekiel and Mindel, 37
Bronfman, Harry, 37
Bronfman, Saidye (nee Rosner), 23
Bronfman, Sam, 23, 37
Brookside Cemetary, 29
Brown, James M., 100, 103

Buller, James, 35
Bun's Master Bakery, 111
Bundy, Ted, 65
Bunn King Bakeries Ltd., 113
Burchill, John, 19

B

Calgary, 7, 8, 89, 119
California, 28, 41
California, 41, 46, 89
Cameron, Lt.-Governor Sir Douglas, 25
Canada Development Corp., 105
Capone, Al, 36, 38
Carlisle, Allan C., 65
Carlton St., 68
Carman, 89
Catholic, 38, 51, 79, 80
Chalmers Community Club, 126
Chaney, Lon, 62
Chicago, 35, 36, 38, 40, 51
Chretien, Prime Minister Jean, 140
Christmas, 45, 69, 75, 76, 82, 127, 129,
Church Ave., 99
Churchill Forest Industries, 92-108
Chwialkowska, Linda, 140
Cincinnati, 113
CKY Television, 68
Clear, Barbara (nee Haliuk), 111, 118-119
Clear, Frances, 118, 119
Clear, Paul, 110-112, 117-120
Clearwater Lake, 125-126
CNR, 32, 61
Colgan, Harold "Bud", 124
Colgan, Lee, 123, 125-128
College Ave., 22, 23
Commission of Inquiry into Churchill Forest Industries, 93-98, 100-102, 104-105
Cornish, Mayor, Francis 7
Cowan, Hugh, 55, 57
Cowan, Lee, 57

Cowan, Lola, 55, 57, 58
Cowan, Margaret, 55
CP Air, 82
CPR, 3, 61
Cross, Const. Robert, 128-138
Cross, Diane, 138
Crystal City, 61
Cuba, 82, 84, 85

D

Dangerfield, George, 117, 118
Danish, 50, 58
De Clerembault Syndrome, 10-13
De Clerembault, Gaetan, 10-13
De Silva, Anthony, 132
Deane, Cyril, 70, 73, 76, 90
Deane, Pauline, 70, 73, 76, 82, 84-85, 90
Demark, Paul, 44
Dillinger, John, 38
Dodds, James, 12
Doerksen, Mary, 18, 24, 26
Donaldson, Clara, 30
Donison, Dawnna, 119-120
Donnelly, Murray S., 105
Douglas, John, FBI profiler, 10, 53, 54
Dowson, Staff Sgt. Ken, 135
Dufferin Ave., 40
Dun and Bradstreet, 98
Dunn, Const. Mary, 30
Dyck, William, 24

E

East Kildonan, 87, 116
Elgin Ave., 129
Ellice Ave., 42, 69
Ellis, Arthur (hangman), 64, 79-80
Elma, 46
Elmwood Cemetary, 59-59
Elmwood, 20, 51, 57, 126
Emerson, 37

England, 19, 60, 66, 79
Enns, Judge John, 134
Eriksdale, 71
Evans, Gurney, 92

F

Federal Bureau of Investigation, 10, 53, 54
fetal alcohol syndrome, 62
Filipino Students Association, 126
First Nation people, 122
Flin Flon, 108
Fort St., 12, 68
Fowlie, Vern, 105
French, 22, 43, 80
Friend, RCMP Const. John, 87

G

gangster, 34, 36, 38, 39
Garry St., 40
Gary, Indiana, 85-86
German, 16, 17, 22, 23
Gessner, Charles, 99
Gilbert St., 99
Gillmor, Don, 130
Gimble, Howard, 43-44
Gindin, Jeff, 120
Glesby, Brian, 99
Glesby, Rose, 99
Glowacki, Wayne, 117
Glueck, Sheldon and Eleanor, 54
Godfrey, Ron, 13
Grand Trunk Pacific Railway, 21
Gray, Harry, 16
Gray, James H., 16, 37
Great Depression, 33, 55
Greek, 86, 118
Grenkow, Paul, 77, 78, 83, 84
Grenkow, Richard, 77, 78, 81, 83, 84, 89
Gretna, 40
Grey, MPP Const. Wilton, 60

Grose, Rex, 94-97, 102-104, 107
Gusenberg, Frank, 36

H

Hagel, Percy, 23
Hale, Lloyd, 105
Haliuk, Dan, 118
Haliuk, Margaret, 112, 118
Hallgrimson, Leifur, 107
Hamilton, Mr. Justice A.C., 134
Handsford, Const. Helen, 30
Harper, Eva, 88
Harper, John Joseph, 128-138
Harper, Lois, 129
Hart, Insp. Shelly, 30
Hartford Ave., 99
Hawthorne, Ave., 45
Headingley Correctional Institution, 79, 84, 136, 139
Headingley, RM of, 59, 136
Heeney, Rev. Berthal, 29
Hespeler Ave., 58
Higgins Ave., 46, 79
Hill, Catherine, 51, 58
Hill, John, 51
Hodgins, Const. Kathryn, 130, 131, 134
Home St., 12, 64
Horwood, V.W., 25
Hot Springs, Arkansas, 25, 41
Houghton, Jim, 124-126, 128
Howell, Manitoba Chief Justice, 29
Hudson, A.B., 25
Hurd, Allan, 99
Hurd, Michael, 99

I

Imperial Bank of Commerce, 87
Ingram, Winnipeg Police Chief John C., 7-8
Institute for Child Health, London, England, 66
Ireland, 57

Island Lake, 129
Island Lakes, 129

J

J.R. Simplot Co., 102
Jack the Ripper, 59
Jesus Christ, 10, 86, 65
Jewish, 22, 23, 28, 38, 43, 45, 98
Johnson, T.H., 25
Johnston, Dwayne Archie, 125-128
Johns-Wride, Esther, 116
Juba, Mayor Steve, 68, 57

K

Kasser, Alexander, 91-108
Kasser, Ivan Michael, 105, 108
Keewatin St., 111, 117, 120, 128
Kehler, Anna, 10
Kehler, J., 44
Kid Cann, 39
Kildonan Dr., 45-46
Kildonan Park, 70
Killarney, 60, 61
Kircaldy, Brandon Police Chief James, 3, 4, 6
Kniver Ave., 111
Knowler, Syd, 42
Kola, 3
Krafchenko, Eli
Krafchenko, John "Jack", 15-29
Kramer, Reinhold, 2, 4, 5, 9, 10, 11, 13
Kreschkoski, Thomas, 46
Krier, Joe, 81
Kuxhaus, David, 136

L

Labatt's Brewery, 111
Lakeview Restaurant, 89
Lane, Mary (nee Robinson), 2-5, 10, 11, 13, 14
Lane, Robert 2-6, 9, 11, 13, 14
Lansky, Meyer, 43

Laurier, Prime Minister Wilfrid, 5-6
Law Enforcement Review Agency, 133, 137-138
Lees, Lawrence, 58
Leishman, Robert, 89
Leishman, Blair, 73, 81, 82, 83, 85, 89, 90
Leishman, Bob, 88
Leishman, Dale, 89
Leishman, Elva (nee Shields), 73-76, 85, 88, 89
Leishman, Ken, 67-90
Leishman, Lee Anne, 74, 76, 83, 89
Leishman, Ron, 83-86, 89-90
Leishman, Trent, 88, 89
Leishman, Wade, 88, 89
Lepine, Ambroise, 7
Letkeman, Dave, 44
Libau, 32, 76
Lichtenstein, 92, 100
Liss Road, 99
Loblaws, 81
Lockport, 99
Loewen, Dr. Linda, 134
Logan Ave., 33, 43, 131
Lombard Ave., 35
Lubosh, Mark, 70
Lucas, Dwight Douglas, 99

M

Ma Barker, 38
MacDonald, Manitoba Premier Hugh John, 25
Machine Gun Kelly, 38
Machine Industries, 74, 88
Machray, John, 56
MacIver, Winnipeg Police Chief, 64
Main St. (Winnipeg), 35, 37, 60, 79, 85, 99
Main, Kelly, 76, 86, 88
Manfor, 107
Manger, Norm, 124, 128
Manitoba Development Fund, 93-98, 100-102
Manitoba Free Press, 9, 11, 14, 17, 18, 19, 23, 24, 26, 27, 29, 36, 43, 49, 60, 61, 63, 65

Manitoba Law Society, 102, 120
Manitoba Legislative Building, 25
Manitoba Liquor Control Commission, 113, 124
Manitoba Mounted Police, 35
Manitoba Provincial Police, 35, 60, 61
Maples, The, 111
Mark Pearce Ave., 70
Marlborough Hotel, 37
Matheson, Glen, 13
Matoff, Paul, 40
McClung, Nellie, 18
McCord, William and Joan, 54-55
McCurdy, Const. Alex, 35
McGavin, Darren, 90
McGirl, Frank, 45
McGregor St., 40
McGregor, Roy Ewan, 64
McIlvride, Alexander, 14
McIver, Don, 127-128
Mckay, Dr. Marilyn, 137-138
McPherson, Wpg. Police Chief Donald, 28
McPhillips Ave., 33
Mecum, Burt, 20
Mecum, Charles, 20
Medley, Henry Medley, 22, 23-24
Meekis, Jackie, 88
Mennonite, 10, 18, 22, 23, 43
Mercury Bay, 132
Metis, 51, 92
Michigan, 36
Minnesota, 38, 39, 40, 43
Minto St., 7
Minto, Governor General Gilbert John, 5, 9
Mitchell, Leon, 105
Mitchell, Tom, 2, 4, 5, 6, 9, 10, 11, 13
Mochary, Mary V., 108
Moggey, Percy, 71-72
Monnin, Mr. Justice Michel, 120
Monoca, A.G., 93-96, 105
Montreal, 37

Moosehorn, 71
Morality Division, 30
Moran, George "Bugs", 36
Morden, 19, 22, 23
Morgan, Leslie, 60
Morin, Det. Sgt. Ronald, 119
Mormon, 83, 84, 86, 89
Morrison, William, 52-53, 62
Mortenson, Bernard, 58
Mourant, Jules, 45
Mulvey School, 57, 58-59
Murray, David B., 7
Murray, Mrs. H.C., 49-50

N

National Post, 140
Nelson, Baby Face, 38
Nelson, Earle aliases, 50
Nelson, Earle, 47-66
New Jersey, 36, 92, 95, 98, 107, 108
New York City, 19, 50, 113, 115
Newman, Walter C., 95, 96, 101-103
Niederhoffer, Arthur and Elaine, 113
Nielsen, Const. Barry Craig, 112-113, 116-120
Nielsen, Diana (nee Haliuk), 112, 118-119
NORAD, 85
North Dakota, 36, 39, 40
North Kildonan, 45, 70, 76, 81, 83
North-West Mounted Police, 7, 35
Norway House First Nation, 123, 124
Notre Dame Ave., 42, 111

O

O'Brien, David, 112, 119
Obee's Steam Baths, 40
Oliphant, Assoc. Chief Justice Jeffrey, 132
Ontario, 21, 27, 46, 51, 75, 76, 77, 78, 83, 88, 89
Osborne St., 33
Osborne, Helen Betty, 121-128, 133, 139
Osborne, Joe, 124

Osborne, Justine, 124
Ottawa, 24, 29, 78

P

Pacific Ave., 128
Paddle Wheel Restaurant, 81
Palay, Abe, 40
Pandora Ave., 27
Patterson, Emily, 57-61, 65
Patterson, William, 57-59
Pembina Highway, 113
Penner, Dorothy, 24-25
Perrault, Martha, 79
Philadelphia, 50, 51, 116
Playgreen Cres., 111
Plum Coulee, 16, 19, 22-24, 26-29
Polish, 43
Portage Ave., 43, 68, 113
Portage la Prairie, 71
Power, Police Chief Richard, 35
Prairie Grove, 44
Presybterian, 7
Priest, Lisa, 123, 125, 127
Prince Albert Penitentiary, 19
Pritchard Ave., 33, 40
Prohibition, 32-46
Prostitution, 7, 30, 59
Proulx, Albert, 87
Pruden, Melvin, 128, 131
psychological profiling, 10, 52, 53

Q

Queens College, 50, 66

R

Radford and Wright warehouse, 12
Rainbow Stage, 70, 98, 107,
Red Lake Chamber of Commerce, 88
Red Lake District News, 75, 84
Red Lake Museum, 89

Red Lake, Ontario, 75-78, 88-89
Reichert, John , 28
Reid, Const. Robert, 23
Reiser, Oscar, 94, 105
Renton, MPP Const. William, 61
Repap Enterprises, 105, 108
Ressler, Robert, FBI profiler, 54
Reston, 33
Richards, RCMP Const. Allen, 83
Riding Mountain National Park, 58
Riel, Louis, 7, 51
Ritchie, James, 36-37
River Ave., 20
Riverton Ave., 57
Riverview, 68, 78, 93
Robertson, Heather, 77, 88
Robinson, John and Anne, 14
Roblin, Manitoba Premier Duff, 25, 57, 93-96,
    102, 105, 107
Roblin, Manitoba Premier Rodmond P., 14, 25
Rolph, Ben, 17, 27
Romania, 16, 19, 27, 28
Rosner, Sam, 23, 28
Rothschild, Maurice, 40
Royal Canadian Mint, 77
Royal Canadian Mounted Police, 16, 38, 43, 44,
    77, 82, 84, 85, 87, 122, 123, 126, 127
Russell, Frances William, 37
Russia, 39
Russian Steam Baths, 40
Russian, 16, 19
Ryan, Tommy, 16, 19

S

Salter St., 39
Salvation Army, 45
San Franciso, 49-51, 60
Saskatchewan, 16, 17, 19, 35, 36, 37, 40, 48, 49,
    50, 60, 72, 74, 79, 94, 137, 139
Saturday Night Magazine, 130

Schechter, Harold, 50, 61, 66
Schreyer, Manitoba Premier Ed, 93, 101, 104
Schroeder, Attorney General Vic, 134
Schultz, Lady, 51
Schultz, Manitoba Lt. Governor Sir John Christian, 51
Scollin, Mr. Justice John, 119
Scopes, John, 62
Scotland Yard, 117
Scotland, 12
Scott, Thomas, 7
Scottish, 22, 43, 73
Second World War, 33
serial killers, 48, 49, 53, 54, 61, 62
Sewell, MPP Const., 60
Shapira, Jack, 98, 107
Sharpe, Frederick, 56
Shaw, Robert, 42,
Shilliday, Gregg, 112
Sifton, Clifford
Sinclair, Associate Chief Judge Murray, 134
Sinclair, Gordon, 134, 137-138
Sitar, Martin, 46
Skolnick, Jerome, 113
Skoog, Doug, 113, 115, 117
Smit, Rick, 75, 84, 86, 88, 89
Smith St., 51, 57
Smith, C. Rhodes, 105
Smith, George, 64
Smith, Pearl, 16, 19
Smith, Winnipeg Police Chief George, 57, 59, 60-61
Smyth, Const. Dan, 133
Somerset, 73
Sophonow, Thomas, 114
South Africa, 24
Spain, Bertrand John Patrick, 24
Spivak, Sydney, 96
Springfield, RM of, 38
St. Boniface, 33, 35, 43, 51, 114

St. John's College, 22
St. Paul's High School, 130
St. Valentine's Day Massacre, 36
Stanley, RCMP Sgt. Ed, 87
Stark, Philip, 61
Ste. Anne, 44
Ste. Anne's Rd., 44
Steinbach, 43, 44, 85, 111
Stephen, Police Chief Herb, 111, 133
Stewart, Alfred P., 3, 6
stills, 32, 33, 37, 38
Stolar, Const. Jerry Carl, 113, 116-120
Stonewall, 24, 44, 115
Stoney, Walter, 79-80
Stony Mountain Penitentiary, 21, 44, 45, 71, 72, 75, 76, 77, 83, 84, 88, 106
Stoppel, Barbara, 114
Strangler, 47-66
Stripp, Emma, 11
Sundown, 37
Supreme Court of Canada, 114, 119
Swiss banks, 92, 100
Swiss, 93, 94
Switzerland, 95, 98, 100, 105

T

Tache Ave., 33
Taylor, Port Arthur Police Chief George, 64
Technopulp companies, 95
Tessler, Corp. Joe, 87
Teulon, 71
The Bay store, 69
The Pas, 92-93, 95, 97, 101, 103-105, 107-108, 122-124, 126
Third St. (The Pas), 125
Thomas Kelly & Sons, 25
Thompson, 108
Thunder Bay, Ont., 88-89
Timlock, Jack, 98
Toews, Abraham, 44

Toews, Bernard, 10
Toews, Heinrich A., 10
Tolko Industries (Tolk Manitoba Inc.), 108
Tolstoi, 33, 37, 40
Torgrud, Ray, 68
Transair, 77, 78, 81
Transcona, 27, 32
Traynor, Const. William, 20
Treherne, 73, 81
Turtle Mountains, 36-37

U

U.S. Securities and Exchange Commission, 95, 105
Ukrainian, 16, 19, 22, 37, 43
University of Manitoba, 56, 69, 126
University of Winnipeg, 52, 113
University Place, 55
Urbanski, Const. Bob, 127-128
Uttley, Const. James, 35

V

Vancouver, 41, 46, 82
Vargas, Eric, 126
Vargha-Khadem, Faraneh, 66
Vaughan St., 55
Vaughan Street Jail, 29, 79, 85
Vescio, Michael, 64
Villiers, Frank, 35
Vimy Park, 119
Vincent, James, 24
Viscount Gort Hotel, 69
Vita, 37
Vivian, 87

W

Wapoka, 60
Warren, 84
Wasagamack, 129
Webb, Winnipeg Mayor Ralph, 37

Weber, Max, 86
Weinstein, Hymie, 120
Weir, Manitoba Premier Walter, 96
Weiss, Hymie, 38
West Kildonan, 99
Westbrook Hotel, 128-130
Whitechapel District, 59
Wilson, Gerald, 127
Winkler, 19
Winks St., 130
Winnipeg Fire Department, 12
Winnipeg Free Press, 68, 69, 78, 85, 94, 103, 105, 107, 108, 112, 116, 117, 118, 119, 136
Winnipeg International Airport, 69, 70, 76, 77, 82
Winnipeg Police Jail, 17, 23
Winnipeg Police, 12, 17, 19, 20, 30, 58, 59, 60, 64, 71, 88, 106, 113, 114, 129, 132
Winnipeg Sun, 112
Winnipeg Telegram, 5, 17, 18, 19
Winnipeg Tribune, 65
Winnipeg's North End, 22, 33
Wolch, Harry, 117, 118
Wolchock, Archibald William, 31-46
Wolchock, Leonard, 32-46
Wolchock, Rose, 41, 45
Women's Christian Temperance Union, 11
World War One, 48
Wride, Dean Eric, 116
Wright, Ernie and Christina, 132
Wright, Tammy, 132
X-Men, 115
Yeomans, Dr. Amelia, 11, 13, 14
York Ave., 51, 55
Zacharias, Staff Sgt. Menno, 135
Zakopiac, Alexander, 87
Zeigler, James, 103
Zola, Irving, 54, 55